"Treat yourself to this heartwarming and deeply relatable look into the challenges and blessings of everyday life through the lens of faith in the God of the Bible. Each chapter is a 'snapshot,' blending humor, wisdom, and personal experience to address life's ups and downs, from family struggles to moments of unexpected joy written by my longtime friend Kathy Christopher. This book is a valuable resource for anyone seeking hope, resilience, and a renewed perspective on life's journey."

— Tom Hughes, Pastor Christian Assembly Church in Los Angeles, Author of *Curious* and *Down to Earth*.

"*Snapshots: Everyday Lessons from a Life of Faith* is a collection of short stories that generously offer wisdom and love on each and every page. The stories are practical, faith-filled, and like Kathy writes, they 'will give you a handhold to grasp and a light to follow toward freedom.' I highly recommend this beautiful book."

— Juli Boit, Founder Living Room International, Author of *From Beyond the Skies* and *Brave Love*

"In her book, *Snapshots: Everyday Lessons from a Life of Faith*, Kathy Christopher shares some of the most sincere lessons accumulated over her life as a daughter, a wife, a mother, a widow, a Pastor and as a "Sinner Saved by Grace". She has a way of bringing lessons alive and focused on the deeper things God reveals to us in the scriptures. I think you will be blessed as I have been when you spend a few minutes a day and meditate on these gifted devotional thoughts."

— Dr. Terry J. Woychowski, Author of *The Energy to Lead, the Thermodynamics of Leadership,* CEO Level V Advising LLC, President, Caresoft Global

"*Snapshots* is such a gift, and each one with a lesson to ponder and apply. Kathy is the best, because she leads the way with her own honesty. No cover ups. If you are stuck, *Snapshots* will help you get unstuck. Do yourself a favor."

— Mark Pickerill, Pastor Emeritus Christian Assembly Church in Los Angeles

"I have known my dear friend Kathy Christopher for over 30 years. She's one of those people, that if you get to sit and have a chat with her you will feel happy, inspired and challenged all at the same time. Reading *Snapshotss* is like having a coffee with her and gaining all of the above."

— Tommy Walker, Worship Leader, Songwriter, Author

"I just finished reading the last 'Snapshot.' I've been using them as daily devotionals, and oh, my—I will miss them. Snapshots are Bible-based down-to-earth nuggets that offer healing, humor and heart. This book is a blessing. I highly recommend it."

— Connie Averitt Williams, Author of *Ants Across the Page*

SNAPSHOTS

Everyday lessons from a life of faith

by

KATHY CHRISTOPHER

Snapshots: Everyday lessons from a life of faith

Cover Design by Karley Carrillo
Typesetting by riverdesignbooks.com

Illustrations by Sherry Barrett, Connie Chandler, Kim MacDonald, Renee Taylor

Paperback ISBN: 979-8-218502-81-2
Ebook ISBN: 979-8-218624-79-8

All Bible references are taken from the New Living Translation version unless otherwise noted.

Dedication

I have many people I love and who love me, who have been instrumental in seeing this project through to publication. Yet I can only dedicate this book to the One who authored every story, brought healing through its truth, and birthed this book in my heart.

Thank you, Loving Father, for trusting me with it.

Contents

Introduction

I sat in my office at the church across from a young wife and mother who was at the end of her rope. She was tired and overwhelmed by life—housekeeping, finances, parenting, marriage—and she didn't know where to turn. A picture came to mind (that happens to me a lot) of a giant pile of laundry next to a very small washing machine. Clearly that mound would not fit in that washer. What to do? Sort the laundry into smaller piles, I advised this young mom. We then went on to talk about what that might look like in her busy life. It may sound obvious to some, but when we're in the thick of it we can lose perspective. A snapshot offered her a way through, a way toward peace.

If I could manage it, I would sit with you in a coffee shop, hear your story, and talk about God's love and wisdom available to you. That's what this book is, a collection of snapshots, in both visual and story form, that are, as a whole, quite practical. Life can be messy and complicated, and I believe we need more guidance than simply being told to "pray about it." Yes, praying is vital to living our best life, but God has also given us Scripture and a brain and encourages us to use them. Whether you are struggling with your faith, your family, or your inner world, these stories will give you a handhold to grasp and a light to follow toward freedom.

These stories are not just words on a page—they come from a life filled with real struggles, joys, discoveries, and faith. As the child of a single mom, I was raised in church and loved Jesus from an early age. My father was mostly absent and an alcoholic, and my grandfather, also an alcoholic, was domineering and abusive—verbally, emotionally and sexually. As an adult, I have struggled in my everyday faith just like many of you. Whether it was in my marriage and subsequent loss of my beloved husband, or in my on-and-off battle with weight. But I've seen God rescue and redeem me time and again. And, having served as one of the pastors at Christian Assembly Church in Los Angeles for almost thirty years, I've also seen God's faithfulness with the thousands of people I had the honor of teaching and counseling.

Many of these Snapshots were birthed in those encounters. I am a visual learner and understand best through images and stories. Sometimes a picture would come to mind as I was trying to grasp a new truth or in conversation with someone needing help and direction, like *Tokens of Influence*. Occasionally the images come from a real life situation that reflects an important truth, like *Sacred French Fries.* My artist friend, Sherry Barrett, did the bulk of the images as she listened to my word pictures and turned them into art. Some Snapshots are strange and require explanation while others are clear and simple. I started collecting them years ago and have seen many people touched by these stories, watching their lives grow in beautiful ways. I want that for all of us, and now feel the need to put this collection into print. I've written them the way I talk: casual, sometimes sarcastic or funny, sometimes difficult, and always honest and direct. I pray that each, along with the accompanying scriptures, create a tapestry of understanding, practical help, and light for your journey of faith. At the end you'll find a topical index for those who wish to find specific snapshot themes.

At the heart of it, I want this book to offer you hope. Now in my 70s, I live pretty much in peace and security. A peace I have had to fight for through my brokenness, lack of healthy coping skills, and a challenging marriage. Trust me, I'm not dishing out advice from a mountain top! I've lived, and sometimes still find myself, in the trenches. Life throws us difficult circumstances that we cannot control, but we can control how we will respond. And the way we respond usually determines who we are becoming.

Be assured that whatever you have faced or are facing, I know from experience that God cares and has a redeeming plan for you. I pray that any wisdom you gain in these pages will be both spiritual and deeply human as you find the message trustworthy, practical, and authentic.

PS: If you have never experienced a loving relationship with God or have given up on the idea of God or 'religion' or faith, I have included at the back of the book a simple explanation of what I believe about God and His love for you.

Chapter 1

A Snapshot of….

A Gracious Spill

I officiated a fun wedding at the filming site for the TV show, *Dr. Quinn, Medicine Woman*. The wedding was western themed, and the reception was held in an open-air barn with barbecue, potato salad, and all the fixings for an Old West party. At one point, the bride stopped by my table to thank me for doing the ceremony. Apparently, I was "Awesome!" (her words, which I share here with great humility). While we were speaking, her very happy husband joined her carrying a plate laden with food. As he put his arm around her, it tipped, spilling baked beans down the front of her pristine white dress. Time stopped. Conversation stopped. Breathing stopped. The groom stared. We all stared. The bride, after the initial shock, looked up at him with a smile and said it was okay, "No worries." The mother of the bride quickly intervened with a two-liter bottle of club soda and a trip to the ladies' room. A short while later the bride was on the dance floor with her husband, no visible traces of BBQ on her beautiful dress.

The spilled beans are a fitting metaphor for how we impact the people with whom we come in contact. What we carry inside spills out when we are bumped, jostled, or distracted. A driver takes liberties in front of us, someone fails to understand our point of view; countless things, large and small, can trigger our emotional response. Our reactions reflect what is inside us: fear or peace, anger or kindness, generosity or selfishness, grace or retaliation. Had the groom spilled a glass of club soda on his bride's dress it would hardly be remembered. But the baked beans on her white satin dress revealed someone filled with grace, patience, and sanity even in an uncomfortable, embarrassing situation. Her true nature spilled out and onto her new husband.

What is it that spills onto others when you are offended, hurt, or confronted? Sadly, the people who most often bump into us are those in our closest circle: spouse, children, close friends and parents. The very people we have committed to love and protect can be scarred by our toxic spills. No one chooses to hurt the ones they love but it happens anyway. The answer is not just to keep the anger inside and swallow our painful emotions. Rather, it is to deal with what is in our cup...our glass...our heart. That is not an easy assignment, but it

is one that can change the quality of your life as well as the lives of those around you.

We all carry the scars of pain, disappointment, and loss in life. We fail others and we fail ourselves. I'm not saying we are awful; I know too many great people to believe that. But most of us have been touched by pain and loss that can sometimes breed fear, resentment, insecurity, pride and so much more. It's not a pretty list. We don't always get to choose what happens to us, but we do choose how we will respond, and those responses show what's in our hearts, minds, and attitudes.

I grew up in severe poverty. My father, an alcoholic, was gone more than he was present. My maternal grandfather was an alcoholic who was an abuser to his children and grandchildren (physical, emotional, and sexual). My mom worked at least two jobs at a time to raise her three daughters. It was a very difficult life for her, but Mom was not bitter, hard, or angry. She was a gentle, caring, kind person right up to her death at ninety-one. How did she do that? When I was three, Mom was invited to church by a neighbor, found Jesus's love and compassion, and lived her life choosing to love and forgive. She couldn't control what happened to her, but she chose to live out of the love of God that filled her heart. When my mom was bumped or jostled, love spilled out.

Each day we can make choices that lead to life and health rather than bitterness and hurt. God offers us love, joy, peace, patience, kindness, goodness, faithfulness, gentleness, and self-control—what the Bible calls the fruit, or result, of God's Spirit in us (Gal. 5:22-23). In my experience, our very best life, our sweetest and fullest cup, comes only through relationship with Jesus. We can never be grace-givers until we begin to grasp the grace that has come to us.

So, what fills your heart, mind and soul? What spills out from you when people bump into you? Will they remember the encounter with a sense of hope and peace? Or will you be the story of the worst part of their day. The good news is, you get to choose.

Further Reading

Romans 3:23-24 *Since we've compiled this long and sorry record as sinners (both us and them) and proved that we are utterly incapable of living the glorious lives God wills for us, God did it for us. Out of sheer generosity he put us in right standing with himself. A pure gift. He got us out of the mess we're in and restored us to where he always wanted us to be. And he did it by means of Jesus Christ.*

Titus 3:3-7 *Once we, too, were foolish and disobedient. We were misled and became slaves to many lusts and pleasures. Our lives were full of evil and envy, and we hated each other. But when God our Savior revealed his kindness and love, he saved us, not because of the righteous things we had done, but because of his mercy. He washed away our sins, giving us a new birth and new life through the Holy Spirit. He generously poured out the Spirit upon us through Jesus Christ our Savior. Because of his grace he made us right in his sight and gave us confidence that we will inherit eternal life.*

John 10:10 *The thief's [Enemy] purpose is to steal and kill and destroy. My purpose is to give them a rich and satisfying life.*

Ezekiel 36:26 *And I will give you a new heart, and I will put a new spirit in you. I will take out your stony, stubborn heart and give you a tender, responsive heart.*

Genesis 1-3

Worth Reading

The Ragamuffin Gospel: Good News for the Bedraggled, Beat-Up, and Burnt Out by Brennan Manning

Abba's Child: The Cry of the Heart for Intimate Belonging by Brennan Manning

[Attitude, Grace, Influence]

Chapter 2

A Snapshot of….

UNEXPECTED JOY!

My Uncle Don is an adventurer, a helper, a problem solver, and a hoot. He and my Aunt Candace retired years ago from law enforcement jobs and have been on a grand adventure ever since. Exceptional at making friends, they once trekked across Australia in an RV for six months in order to see the country and get to know the people. They have formed pickleball clubs in every city where they've lived in the last twenty years, just for fun and connection. Other adventures include volunteering with the Red Cross in New York after 9/11 and working security at the Atlanta Olympics. Everywhere they go, they leave that place better than they found it.

In 1991 they wanted to experience Russia so traveled there with a tour group. At the end of their trip, they found themselves stuck in the Moscow airport: snowed in, no flights out, stranded along with hundreds of others from all over the world. Bodies were strewn over chairs, floors, and one another. Bathrooms were ill-equipped to handle the mass of people and deemed "disgusting and unusable," in my uncle's words. Unlike our modern major airports today, there were no restaurants and the few small kiosk markets at the time were closed. Everyone was tired, hungry, uncomfortable, and very unhappy.

My aunt and uncle live by the philosophy that situations like this are not inconveniences but opportunities. This isn't just a bumper sticker or tag line for them, they really do live it. For example, Uncle Don always carries balloons in his pocket. "You just never know when you'll need them."

So, on this captive snow-bound day, amid the hundreds of disgruntled and miserable adults and children, Uncle Don, walking through the rows of people, blew up a balloon and pinched the neck of it to slowly let air out in a high-pitched squeal. When he had peoples' attention, he blew up the balloon again, tied it off and hit it into the air, because, as he says, "People cannot resist keeping a balloon from hitting the floor." Once that section was busy with their balloon he walked to another section and repeated the process. Ultimately, he had about ten balloons in the air. People would jump up or bat them around and soon most of these unhappy and even angry people were laughing and working together to keep their balloon aloft. Kids who had been lying on the floor or whining were now squealing with delight and chasing the colorful, bouncing joy-bringers. A simple, extremely cheap novelty item changed everything for a sea of international travelers stranded in an overcrowded, snowbound airport in Moscow, Russia.

There are plenty of reasons to be upset, angry, disgusted and worried, but we don't have to be. We get to choose how we respond to the stuff of life. When you show up, whether to a party or a problem, do you feed the anger, sadness, or discomfort, or do you bring peace and joy? Are you prone to assess the quality of your life solely by your circumstances or by the opportunities you have to choose gratitude? Do you move through life with your pockets filled with kindness, patience, grace, and joy, like my Uncle Don's balloons? If so, there will always be plenty of opportunities to use them.

It's as easy as making a choice, as simple as approaching the circumstances of your life with the intention to bring goodness. It can be as simple as tossing a balloon in the air.

Further Reading

Matthew 5:9 *God blesses those who work for peace, for they will be called the children of God.*

James 1:2 *Dear brothers and sisters, when troubles of any kind come your way, consider it an opportunity for great joy.*

Proverbs 12:20 *Deceit fills hearts that are plotting evil; joy fills hearts that are planning peace!*

Philippians 3:1a MSG *And that's about it, friends. Be glad in God!*

Philippians 4:4 *Always be full of joy in the Lord. I say it again—rejoice!*

[Attitude, Choices, Joy]

Chapter 3

A Snapshot of….

GREAT WINE

The concept of turning water into wine has been mentioned in books, movies, TV, and certainly innumerable conversations. Taking something common and plentiful and changing it into something extraordinary is an appealing idea. You may know that the basis for this phenomenon is a first-century Palestinian wedding story told in the Bible. A young Jewish man named Jesus was at a wedding with His mom and His friends. He was minding His own business when His mother approached Him with the terrible news: they were running out of wine. Unfortunate, but not a major catastrophe, right?

In ancient Jewish culture it was not just embarrassing to run out of food or drink for the guests, it was shaming. Some historians have suggested that it was an offense worthy of legal action! Can you imagine getting sued by a guest at your wedding because you ran out of chicken? It's difficult to imagine such a thing in today's world, we would just run over to Trader Joe's Market and get what we needed. In this ancient story, however, whether it was limitations of finance or product, there was no such quick solution to the lack of wine, and that could ruin a wedding.

Jesus's mother, Mary, is likely involved in helping facilitate the wedding as she appears to be one of the first to know the wine is running out. Her response is immediate as she tells the servants, "Whatever he says to do, do it." I wish I could have seen Jesus's face when He asks, "What are you talking about, Mother?" Ultimately, He agrees and directs the servants to fill up the water jars. Which seems odd, right? They aren't out of water! But the servants do as they are told and fill the twenty to thirty-gallon stone jars normally used for ceremonial washing (Jewish ritual). Then Jesus tells them, "Dip out some water and take it to the master of ceremonies." Again, I can only imagine the conversation among the servants…

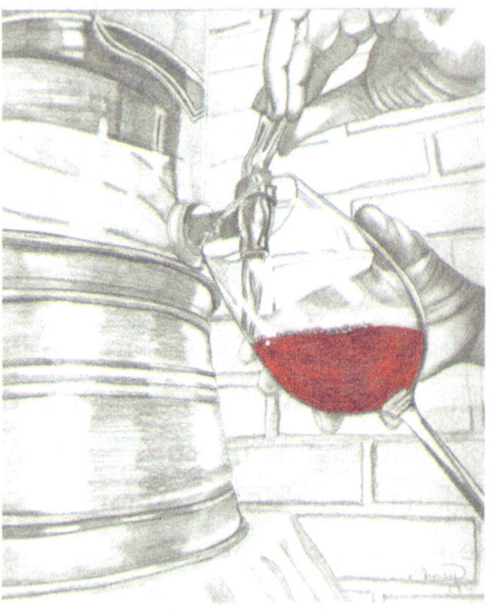

"You take it to him."

"I'm not taking it…you take it!"

"It's water! What if he shoots the messenger?"

In any case, a servant takes the water to the important master of ceremonies who drinks and declares it the best wine of the feast.

In fact, he says that most people get their guests pretty drunk then bring out the cheap stuff, but not here! The very best wine comes later in the day, from a water jug, directed by a man named Jesus.

I am always deeply challenged by this story—this miracle. You see, we don't know when the water became wine. Was it turned into wine in the jar? In the cup? On the way to the host or as he sipped it? It doesn't matter. The details don't change the outcome. Jesus did it and everyone at the wedding benefited, especially the wedding family. How did it happen? Someone chose to trust Jesus and do what He said.

In my long life I have run into countless situations where I did not know what to do. Whether I was gripped with hopelessness, frozen by seeming impossibilities, or barreling down a path toward self-destruction, I had no clue and no plan. These words would echo in my mind and heart, "Whatever he says, do it." I've learned to turn toward God in those moments, whether through the Bible or prayer, usually both, and listen to what He says. And then, most of the time, I do it. I may do it afraid, or with an attitude (shocking, I know), or with very little faith or hope, but I do it. I turn my attention toward my marriage, not away. I ask for forgiveness rather than initiate a defense. I donate rather than accumulate. I'm not always immediate and often not thrilled, but I commit myself again. "Whatever he says, do it."

I can tell you that I have *never* been sorry I followed God's direction. It is seldom easy, but always worth it. I have experienced the miracle of a restored marriage, financial provision, healed relationships, and so much more. I never had to make a miracle, but I did have to trust the One who could. Those times when I knew the right thing to do but chose not to, I have always had regret. But I have never regretted trusting and following God.

If there is an area in your life where you could use a miracle, I encourage you to turn to the One who knows you, loves you, and has the power to make a difference. He is not a magician you ask for a great trick, but He is in the business of making the ordinary things of life extraordinary. He is the God who created you and desires goodness for you. It may not be easy, but it is absolutely worth it.

Further Reading

Psalm 145:17 *The Lord is righteous in everything he does; he is filled with kindness.*

Isaiah 55:8-9 *"My thoughts are nothing like your thoughts," says the Lord. "And my ways are far beyond anything you could imagine. For just as the heavens are higher than the earth, so my ways are higher than your ways and my thoughts higher than your thoughts."*

Hosea 14:10 *Let those who are wise understand these things. Let those with discernment listen carefully. The paths of the Lord are true and right, and righteous people live by walking in them. But in those paths sinners stumble and fall.*

Revelation 15:3-4 *And they were singing the song of Moses, the servant of God, and the song of the Lamb: "Great and* *marvelous are your works, O Lord God, the Almighty. Just and true are your ways, O King of the nations. Who will not fear you, Lord, and glorify your name? For you alone are holy. All nations will come and worship before you, for your righteous deeds have been revealed."*

John 2:1-11 *Three days later there was a wedding in the village of Cana in Galilee. Jesus' mother was there. Jesus and his disciples were guests also. When they started running low on wine at the wedding banquet, Jesus' mother told him, "They're just about out of wine." Jesus said, "Is that any of our business, Mother—yours or mine? This isn't my time. Don't push me." She went ahead anyway, telling the servants, "Whatever he tells you, do it." Six stoneware water pots were there, used by the Jews for ritual washings. Each held twenty to thirty gallons. Jesus ordered the servants, "Fill the pots with water." And they filled them to the brim. "Now fill your pitchers and take them to the host," Jesus said, and they did. When the host tasted the water that had become wine (he didn't know what had just happened but the servants, of course, knew), he called out to the bridegroom, "Everybody I know begins with their finest wines and after the guests have had their fill brings in the cheap stuff. But you've saved the best till now!" This act in Cana of Galilee was the first sign Jesus gave, the first glimpse of his glory. And his disciples believed in him.*

[Choices, Faith, Obedience]

Chapter 4

A Snapshot of....

TOKENS OF INFLUENCE

Have you ever heard a parent harping at their kids? "Sit up straight." "Say please." "Say thank you." "No, you can't have a cookie." It frightens me to think how much I was probably like that when my kids were young. We want them to mature well, but we can become crushing naggers!

It struck me one day that this has something to do with tokens. We each are entrusted with "tokens" to use in the lives of those closest to us. They represent our rules, preferences, opinions, expressed needs, or influence. They are opportunities to speak into another's life, to offer wisdom, correction, or guidance. When kids are very young, we have almost limitless tokens to spend on them. A new baby is utterly dependent for most everything—eating, sleeping, clothing, etc. At two years old, they have more of an opinion about what they eat and perhaps even what they will wear; therefore, you have fewer tokens. At five, even fewer. Teenagers? Forget about it. Maybe two, if you're lucky! When your children are grown, all you really have is a big dose of hope and whatever influence you've developed because of a good relationship with them.

When our son was in high school, he began talking about getting a tattoo or piercing his ear, and I was not a big fan of either. Knowing we had very limited tokens to spend with our seventeen-year-old son, we said no to the tattoo and he opted to get his ear pierced instead. When he was out of college and in the work force, he decided to let the earring go. By that time, I didn't care about the piercing and thought he looked cool with it—I didn't spend a token on that decision! Obviously, as an adult, if he chose to get a tattoo today that's his business. In my relationship with my children today, any token I have is because they hand it to me. I believe this respect comes from learning along the way that we only had a limited number of tokens all along. Mostly, we live in mutual influence with one another. The tokens, though fewer, now begin again with my grandchildren.

This can be a helpful concept in all our relationships. You don't have unlimited tokens with anyone, none of us do, though I've known people who think they do! I am amazed at the number of times this pattern has shown itself in family difficulties: wives trying to control their husband's thoughts or actions, husbands trying to control their wives, parents to children and on it goes. When we desperately try to control or "improve" the other, we are, in essence, spending tokens that are worth nothing. When we overplay our tokens (influence) they lose their value.

I spent years trying to make my husband, Budd, more like me—a woman of God. He didn't respond well. Controlling others is not the road to intimacy and connection. Granted, it is not easy to determine which and how many tokens we possess in any given relationship. But we can earn tokens by trusting the other, encouraging them, and allowing them freedom to be who they are. Being reminded of the limits of our tokens should help us treat others with acceptance and patience.

Carrying this a step further, I think we wrestle with the idea that God truly does have unlimited tokens. He alone knows what is best. Yet we often treat God as though we have graciously allowed Him to spend a few tokens in a certain area of our life, then withhold His right to speak in other areas. I may ask God's guidance in terms of my finances but don't want to know what He has to say about the way I treat other people. I've sometimes refused God's use of tokens in my life. I didn't trust He would be gentle with me, or that surrendering my desires or dreams would leave me with anything to hold on to. I refused His hand offered to me so many times, and still He came to me with grace and kindness. As I have learned to accept His word and His ways (His tokens), my life is more of what I'd always wanted it to be.

The only limit to God's blessing and goodness is our willingness to accept it. God may have a limitless supply of tokens to use for our good, but our openness and receptivity is what allows Him to use them. When we refuse to trust Him, we're like a child poking through Grandpa's handful of change, picking out just the coins we want and rejecting the others, unaware that every single coin has value. How often have I sorted through the promises of God and chosen the ones I thought were best or easiest for me to handle, missing out on so many other life-giving and life-changing promises.

Collectively, God's handful of "tokens" represent your very best life. He really is good; He always knows what is best for you and He delights in loving you.

Take a few moments to consider where you have been spending tokens with people in your life. Are you using your relationship influence wisely? Are you exerting influence for others' good or for your own comfort or control? Does God have influence in your life? This is a good time to ask Him for help and wisdom.

Further Reading

Romans 15:1-2 MSG *Those of us who are strong and able in the faith need to step in and lend a hand to those who falter, and not just do what is most convenient for us. Strength is for service, not status. Each one of us needs to look after the good of the people around us, asking ourselves, "How can I help?"*

Luke 6:31 *Do to others as you would like them to do to you.*

John 15:12 *This is my commandment: Love each other in the same way I have loved you.*

Jeremiah 29:11 *"For I know the plans I have for you," says the LORD. "They are plans for good and not for disaster, to give you a future and a hope."*

Romans 8:38-39 *And I am convinced that nothing can ever separate us from God's love. Neither death nor life, neither angels nor demons, neither our fears for today nor our worries about tomorrow—not even the powers of hell can separate us from God's love. No power in the sky above or in the earth below – indeed, nothing in all creation will ever be able to separate us from the love of God that is revealed in Christ Jesus our Lord.*

[Influence, Parenting, Relationships, Trust]

Chapter 5

A Snapshot of....

DISHES RATTLING

As a single mother of three girls, my mom worked two jobs just to keep a roof over our heads and food in our stomachs. She worked in a high school cafeteria during the day and at a Walgreens drug store soda fountain at night.

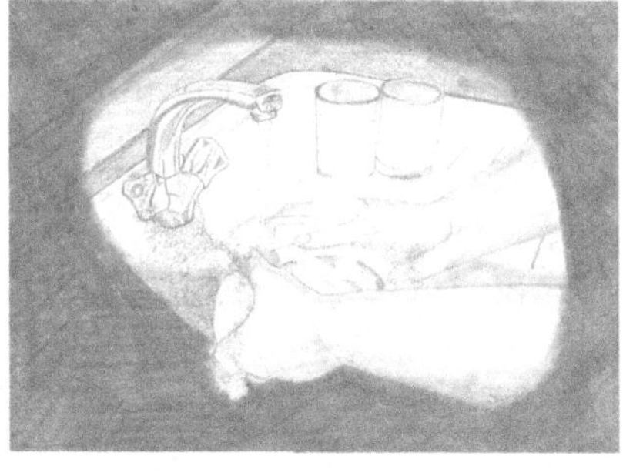

We lived in a few small, rented rooms in a white clapboard house on a dirt road next to the railroad tracks. It was a small town in Illinois at a time when children could play outdoors and roam the neighborhood safely. My sisters and I spent a lot of time watching out for one another with little or no adult supervision, though I was the self-appointed boss of us.

When Mom arrived home from her evening job at 9:30 p.m. we were to be bathed and in bed. On one particularly cold and blustery night, my sisters had fallen asleep quickly after we had crawled into the double bed we shared. I lay awake as a bare branch scratched across the window and its shadow darted around the room in the moonlight like a craggy, clutching hand. I was terrified. I prayed desperately that God would bring Mom home quickly and buried my head under a pillow to drown out the terrifying sights and sounds. Startled suddenly by a sound close by, I slowly lifted the pillow from my head, my heart pounding in my nine-year-old chest. It was dishes rattling in the kitchen. Mom was home. We were not alone, after all. Mom would take care of everything. I snuggled under the blankets, closed my eyes, exhaled, and easily went to sleep.

Several years ago, I was in a very dark season in my life. It was one of those times where I felt alone, anxious, and hopeless. God seemed very distant and deaf to my prayers, and though I tried to hold steady I felt utterly lost. During this dark time, I received a card from a friend I hadn't heard from in years. She wrote that she had been praying for me and wanted me to know that God loved me and she did too. She had no idea what was going on in my life, but wanted me to know that God saw me, heard my prayers, and was very present with me. Her card was a handle for hope. It was the sound of God rattling dishes in the kitchen. I was not alone.

Feeling abandoned, alone, or afraid is not unique to just you or me; it's the human condition. There is a story in the Bible (Mark 4) about Jesus and His friends in a boat crossing the Sea of Galilee. A violent storm came up and they were terrified of sinking and drowning, except for Jesus, of course. He was asleep in the boat.

Asleep. They frantically woke Him saying the equivalent of, "Hey! We're drowning here! Do something!" Jesus told the storm to stop, and it did. The wind and the waves calmed. Cool to imagine, and possibly scary for the guys in the boat.

But God doesn't always end our storms. Sometimes He just holds onto us as the storm blows through. The God who calmed the storm that day in the boat is present with you. If you're in a tough season, ask Him to let you know He's close and taking care of things. He sees you. He knows you. He cares for you. It may not seem like it at the moment, but He is watching over you. When you feel alone, afraid, and even terrified, stop, quiet your mind and heart, and listen. The God who loves you is rattling dishes in your kitchen to let you know He is there, and He will take care of you. Think of someone in your life who could use a bit of encouragement, then take a minute to let them know you care. Rattle a few dishes on God's behalf.

Further Reading

Matthew 11:28-30 MSG *Are you tired? Worn out? Burned out on religion? Come to me. Get away with me and you'll recover your life. I'll show you how to take a real rest. Walk with me and work with me—watch how I do it. Learn the unforced rhythms of grace. I won't lay anything heavy or ill-fitting on you. Keep company with me and you'll learn to live freely and lightly.*

Deuteronomy 31:8 *Do not be afraid or discouraged, for the LORD will personally go ahead of you. He will be with you; he will neither fail you nor abandon you.*

Psalm 40:1-3

I waited patiently for the LORD to help me,
and he turned to me and heard my cry.
He lifted me out of the pit of despair,
out of the mud and the mire.
He set my feet on solid ground
and steadied me as I walked along.
He has given me a new song to sing,
a hymn of praise to our God.
Many will see what he has done and be amazed.
They will put their trust in the LORD.

[Fear, God's Presence, Parenting]

Chapter 6

A Snapshot of....

A Pole of Protection

Years ago, I was talking with a young mom who had a very strong-willed son. Just eight or nine years old at the time, he was convinced he knew best about everything. He was bright, active and seemed destined to be a very good lawyer. She is a gentle soul, loves her children immensely and wanted to do the right thing by them. The slightest directive to her son was answered with resistance, argument, and petulance. She was truly at her wits' end as to how to parent him well. Threatening him with "Wait till your dad gets home" was not the way she wanted to handle it. As we talked, I was struck with a picture.

Growing up in the Midwest many homes had

basements, often used as playrooms or dens. At my friend's house we would play tag, wrestle, and, because it was downstairs, we could go all out with noise and activity. One thing we had to watch out for were the poles that were evenly spaced across the middle of the basement. They were steel and did not budge if you ran headlong into one of them. The pole always won. It had to because it was holding up the house.

As I spoke with this young mom, I shared with her the picture of the basement poles and how important they were for the sake of the home. The key, though, is that most of these poles were padded with gym mats. When you ran into one of them it did not budge but it also didn't crack your head open. The pole still won but it didn't destroy you in the process.

Whether you are a parent, a spouse, a leader, or in some other role that requires you to hold influence over someone else, consider two things: first, the necessity of holding to the important rules that maintain a safe and healthy family, workplace, church, for everyone. Secondly, and as crucial, is the necessity to care for those you lead. Keep in mind that you don't have to bend necessary rules in order to be kind in administering them.

In our various roles in life, we are sometimes called upon to hold steady to what is most important even when those around us challenge our priorities. We may be tempted to bend rules to avoid hurt or anger, but some rules should not be bent or broken. The key is to stand strong in the important things in life, but to do so with kindness. In his book *The Divine Conspiracy* Dallas Willard wrote, "One of the hardest things in the world is to be right and not hurt other people with it." This applies to our kids, our spouses, our friends and any other human being with whom we do life.

One of my favorite verses and truths in the Bible is found in **John 1:14**:

> *The Word became flesh and made his dwelling among us. We have seen his glory, the glory of the one and only Son, who came from the Father, full of grace and truth.*

Jesus came as the perfect balance of grace and truth. He is both the immovable pole that holds the world, and He is encompassed in grace and goodness. His kindness, along with the unwavering truth I can cling to, provide me with the confidence to live my best life even in very difficult times.

Whether within a family, workplace, church or circle of friends, it is chaotic and confusing when there are no stated boundaries or expectations. Have you ever tried to work for someone whose expectations changed daily? It is a minefield; you can never satisfy them. It's the same with families and friends: when right and wrong are at the whim of another's mood, it creates an insecure and fearful existence. What is ignored one day might bring a tirade the next. Living in the truth creates sound boundaries that make life-giving relationships possible.

This balance of grace and truth, of strength with kindness, is vital in our relationships. It is a difficult balance to maintain, but I know the One who holds the balance, and He holds me.

Whether you tend to be a steel pole without a cushion or a cushion without a pole, today is a great day to assess your patterns, choose to do better, and pray for God's help to accomplish it. May your house not fall, and your people not be broken. And may God help us to live with strength and kindness, filled with His grace and His truth.

Further Reading

Psalm 25:5 *Lead me by your truth and teach me, for you are the God who saves me. All day long I put my hope in you.*

Ephesians 4:29 *Don't use foul or abusive language. Let everything you say be good and helpful, so that your words will be an encouragement to those who hear them.*

Proverbs 15:23 *Everyone enjoys a fitting reply; it is wonderful to say the right thing at the right time!*

1 Kings 3:9 *Give me an understanding heart so that I can govern your people well and know the difference between right and wrong. For who by himself is able to govern this great people of yours?*

James 1:5 *If you need wisdom, ask our generous God, and he will give it to you. He will not rebuke you for asking.*

[Parenting, Perseverance, Truth]

Chapter 7

A Snapshot of....

SORTING THE LAUNDRY

My son, Matt, learned to drive through his high school's drivers training program. He was a good driver—for a sixteen-year-old. A few months after he got his license, Budd decided to teach him to drive a standard transmission, the prized '66 Volkswagen. So off went my husband and my son in a beautiful Hallmark moment.

Less than five minutes later, Matt came through the door visibly upset.

"What's wrong, honey?"

"Nothing. I'm just deaf and stupid." And off he strode to his room.

A few moments later Budd came through that same door. "What happened? Did you tell Matt he was deaf and stupid?"

"No, I asked if he was deaf *or* stupid."

Thanks for the clarification.

You see, Matt knew how to drive. He had figured out how to coordinate the gas pedal, brake, and steering wheel, to look ahead while glancing in the rearview mirror, to check side mirrors and use his blinkers. There were a lot of moving parts, but he was certainly mastering them. However, in that '66 VW, two more things were added, the clutch and gear shift, and those two things are not easy to maneuver. I about broke my uncle's neck when he tried to teach me to drive his VW.

Juggle one orange, easy. Now add one more, tricky. Now add another, nope. Isn't this like life? We feel like we're adulting pretty well and then something gets added: a job issue, a family situation, financial, spiritual, mental, emotional—suddenly we feel miserably and completely unable to cope. It can feel as though there is no way forward.

I was speaking with a person who was utterly overwhelmed with almost every facet of their life, and a picture came to mind: a giant mound of laundry sitting next to a tiny washing machine. The laundry was a giant jumble of dirty clothes, linens, denims, and delicates of every color and size. It was not possible to get all that laundry into that tiny machine. The washer was not built or ever intended to handle that enormous load. So, assuming we can't just walk away and buy all new stuff, what do we do?

We sort the laundry; we separate this giant mound into smaller piles that can be handled with the resources we have. Now, we may know how to sort jeans from towels, but how do we sort the laundry that is our life? It all seems important and immediate, and usually overwhelming. Think for a minute of every issue that is currently plaguing you. With each item—each pile of laundry—what is one thing you can do toward neutralizing that issue or stress?

This may all sound a bit simplistic, but in my conversation with this young woman, she went from feeling completely overwhelmed and hopeless to, at minimum, having a plan. There were things she could let go of, some that she could postpone, and others for which she had a helpful tangible step to take toward regaining her sense of balance.

Most of us experience seasons of life where we feel overwhelmed and even hopeless. Using our laundry metaphor, what might it look like to sort through all the piles?

— Let's say the towels represent your home. That's one load. What does my home need? What does it need *right now*? Mow the lawn or call the yard guy, paint that room or get a painter, purge a closet. Get that drippy faucet fixed. Don't try to do it all, but do something. Just one thing to start.

— Denims can represent your job. What is the stressor? What is one thing you can do to reduce that stress? Don't say "nothing," that doesn't help. Do you need to talk to your boss? Fix your attitude? Change your focus? Do one thing.

— I hope you've learned to wash red things separately. If not, you probably have a lot of pink undies. Let's say the red load is finances, because they color everything! What do you need? Balance your bank account, set up a budget, talk to a financial advisor. Don't keep worrying and wallowing, sort the laundry. Do one thing.

— Delicates are those items that must be laundered carefully as they are more fragile. This load represents your personal life, your heart and soul. What are you doing for the health of your heart, mind, and body? Are you taking care of your soul? If not, you probably will never find your life in order. We need to care for our tender inner parts. Do one thing.

There are many more loads, of course. Maybe it's an ex-spouse, struggling adult children, difficult parents, a sour neighbor, physical issues, mental issues, so many things can overwhelm us. Some we can handle, some we need help with, and some we need to let go of, like trashing those ratty old T-shirts or sending that suit to the dry cleaners. I encourage you to sort your laundry, sort your life. You didn't get to this point overnight and it won't get fixed in a day, but you can begin to take back control of your life if you do it steadily and sanely.

In Matthew 6:34 Jesus tells us not to worry. This verse often leaves me feeling a bit fatalistic, like Winnie-the-Pooh's friend Eeyore saying, "Oh bother, tomorrow is going to be as bad as today, or worse, so just keep plugging along..." But this verse is a promise. We are made to live in the present moment—in the wholeness, joy, peace, and purpose of today, not worrying about tomorrow. We will never have more than we can bear, never more than we can carry, if we will trust ourselves and our "laundry" to God's gracious and capable care.

God sees us and He cares. Even though some of what we deal with in this life is the result of our own choices, He does not leave us on our own. God invites us to move close into Him and to learn His ways. He knows what our life is to look like. He knows what we can handle. Sort the laundry. Do one thing.

Further Reading

Matthew 11:28-30 *Then Jesus said, "Come to me, all of you who are weary and carry heavy burdens, and I will give you rest. Take my yoke upon you. Let me teach you, because I am humble and gentle at heart, and you will find rest for your souls. For my yoke is easy to bear, and the burden I give you is light."*

Isaiah 43:2 *When you go through deep waters, I will be with you. When you go through rivers of difficulty, you will not drown. When you walk through the fire of oppression, you will not be burned up; the flames will not consume you.*

Jeremiah 31:3 *Long ago the* Lord *said to Israel: "I have loved you, my people, with an everlasting love. With unfailing love I have drawn you to myself."*

1 John 3:1 *See how very much our Father loves us, for he calls us his children, and that is what we are! But the people who belong to this world don't recognize that we are God's children because they don't know him.*

Lamentations 3:22-23 *The faithful love of the* Lord *never ends! His mercies never cease. Great is his faithfulness; his mercies begin afresh each morning.*

[Choices, Despair, Hope]

Chapter 8

A Snapshot of....

A DUMP TRUCK OF HOPE

I stood in the pediatric Intensive Care Unit at UCLA hospital, at the bedside of a two-year-old boy who lay entwined in cords linked to what looked like science-fiction machines. His eyes closed and his breathing labored, he was so small, so helpless. I loved this boy, and I loved his mother who stood opposite me across the bed. Ryan had undergone a bone marrow transplant to fight the sickle cell disease that had begun to ravage his tiny body.

Juli, Titus, and their children were in the US from Kenya. This bone marrow procedure Ryan and his brother were undergoing was known to be life-threatening, but it was also their only hope. They were all walking a journey of such weight it was hard to imagine *how* they were making it. Ryan seemed to be managing the process, but then his organs began to shut down and he was rushed to ICU. It did not look hopeful.

I stood with tears in my eyes and deep pain in my heart, listening to the foreign sounding hums and beeps around me, looking from this precious little boy to his weary, frightened mama. God, have mercy. God, please intervene.

As the nurse adjusted the countless wires hooked up to Ryan, Juli spoke softly to him, holding him in a sitting position. Ryan's eyes opened dully then seemed to focus on something, and he weakly reached out. Sitting on a table at the foot of his bed was a colorful, plastic dump truck. As Juli held him, I picked up the truck and placed it on the bed in front of Ryan. He smiled. I should say, *He smiled!* because that's how miraculous it felt. I put one ball into the truck. He reached his little hand out and I gave him a ball. He placed it in the truck. Juli and I held our breath as we watched this little boy who seemed to be literally coming back to life. We traded places so Juli could be in front of him and talk to him. I held his frail little body in my hands and wanted to both weep and dance.

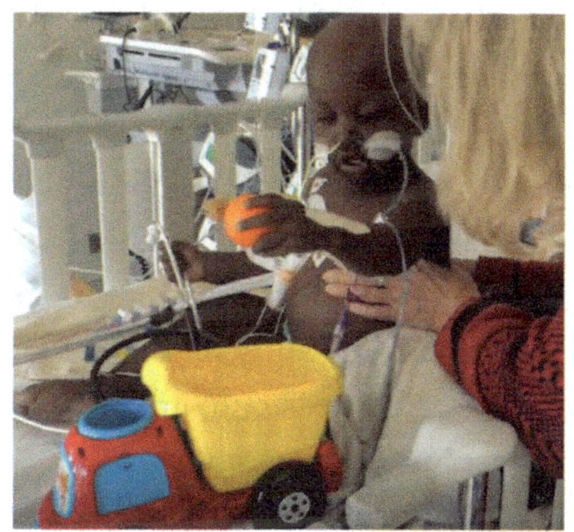

It was a moment in time where hope seeped back into the room, where the sweet scent of joy overrode the antiseptic fear clouding the atmosphere. Ryan was with us, he was alive. It was as though God opened His hands of great mercy and allowed Juli this window into possibilities. There was hope.

Ryan tired quickly and we laid him down again, but the feeling in the room had changed. The colorful little truck was a symbol of promise, of what could be. There were still long days ahead with frightening setbacks and complications. But for about five minutes, in the Pediatric Intensive Care Unit at UCLA Children's Hospital, grace filled a room so acutely that a mom, her son, and a friend inhaled a fresh breath of life.

As it is in every life, there were no guarantees that Ryan would get better, or that he would live. Juli told me countless times that she knew this might not end well. But Juli and Titus believe God is good whatever the outcome. I know that sounds ridiculous to some, but it's a reality for many. Hope is in the goodness of God, not in our perfect outcome. Life happens. *Oy vey.* It just keeps happening.

Today, if you are in challenging or even what feels like hopeless circumstances, I encourage you to pause and consider the idea that God is. God *is.* He is good, He is powerful, He is compassionate, He is wisdom, He is love, He cares more for you than you can imagine. He is. Ask God to give you a glimpse of hope today, a window into who He is and what He can do. It may be as profound as a little boy coming to life or as simple and unexpected as a plastic dump truck. There is no good reason for you to navigate the overwhelming challenges of this life on your own. God is.

Note: The full story of Ryan, Geoffrey, and their sister Sharon, their journey to the US and the bone marrow transplant, is stunningly shared in Juli Boit's book *From Beyond the Skies*. I have read it twice and will read it again.

Further Reading

Lamentations 3:19-24 *The thought of my suffering and homelessness is bitter beyond words. I will never forget this awful time, as I grieve over my loss. Yet I still dare to hope when I remember this: The faithful love of the LORD never ends! His mercies never cease. Great is his faithfulness; his mercies begin afresh each morning. I say to myself, "The LORD is my inheritance; therefore, I will hope in him!"*

Psalm 130:5 *I am counting on the LORD; yes, I am counting on him. I have put my hope in his word.*

Psalm 42:5-6a *Why am I discouraged? Why is my heart so sad? I will put my hope in God! I will praise him again—my Savior and [6] my God! Now I am deeply discouraged, but I will remember you—*

Psalm 33:18-19 *Watch this: God's eye is on those who respect him, the ones who are looking for his love. He's ready to come to their rescue in bad times; in lean times he keeps body and soul together.*

Romans 15:13 *I pray that God, the source of hope, will fill you completely with joy and peace because you trust in him. Then you will overflow with confident hope through the power of the Holy Spirit.*

1 Corinthians 15:19 *And if our hope in Christ is only for this life, we are more to be pitied than anyone in the world.*

[God's Character, Hope, Perseverance, Trust]

Chapter 9

A Snapshot of....

AN INADEQUATE TOOLBOX

I got married when I was twenty-one. Certainly the wisest, most mature and capable twenty-one-year-old to ever enter into matrimony, I had the unbending confidence that I was going to be a great wife. How could I not? I was marrying a guy I met in Bible college! How could our marriage not be great?

Well, marriage was hard! Turns out, Budd wasn't just like me. His cute idiosyncrasies became huge annoyances and offenses against my sensibilities. He was such a...man! We had some rough years. In a time of great despondency and hopelessness there came a picture to my mind:

a toolbox with only two tools in it, a hammer and a pair of pliers. The message it conveyed was that I did not have adequate tools in my toolbox to be married, to be a wife.

I was raised by a single mom, a very good mom. I gained life tools for hard work, loving well, caring for each other, loving Jesus, being thrifty, so many great life tools. What I didn't witness was how to be a wife (single mom, remember?). When I got married, I was unaware that I had no tools for my new role. So, what did I do? I used the tools I had, the ones I'd witnessed my mom using. I parented Budd. I tried to be a good mom to him. Alas, he apparently didn't want that.

It was only by God's grace and a lot of hard work that I began to add tools to my toolbox, by watching marriages I respected, reading helpful books, and a boatload of counseling and prayer. I knew I would not make it without the right tools. And because God is my go-to resource in everything, I began to pray that He would teach me to be a good wife to Budd. Unfortunately, if I can be very honest, God answered my prayer. It was an intensely challenging season of letting go of self-protection, self-defensiveness, self-centeredness, and a whole lot of other self-things. I'm not saying our issues were all my fault, but my side of the marriage was all I could deal with. Gradually, my toolbox began to fill with helpful items like patience, forgiveness, grace, listening and more. It wasn't fast and it wasn't easy, but it was worth it. You see, the tools I gained were not just for my marriage, they were for my best life. I was becoming a person I could appreciate.

I recently purchased a yard blower to help me keep my property presentable. I've watched countless landscape workers blow leaves, dirt, grass, etc. and it looked so cool and easy! So, I broke out my yard blower and immediately sent dirt, leaves, pine needles, and trash into the air, into my face and hair, into the flower bed—everywhere I didn't want it. The more I tried to corral the debris the worse it got. It has taken me quite a while to tame that beast!

The point is, my journey to becoming a better wife was even more challenging. It had much less to do with cooking or cleaning than it did with forgiving, being kind, and adjusting my attitude. It had most to do with bending a knee to God, trusting His guidance, and cooperating as he shaped me—and that last part was not easy! They were difficult tools to master, but they were exactly the tools needed to build my marriage. Assuming I had the right tools didn't work. Refusing to learn to use them didn't work. I needed the right tools and I needed to learn to use them.

We all come into adulthood with limited tools. Life, history, education, family systems, and other factors often fail to provide the necessary tools for our best life. Some may have a better head start on it, but we all need help. Whether it's marriage, parenting, finances, faith, career—wherever you find yourself at a loss for how to succeed—don't give up. Put on your big-kid pants and go after the tools needed for your best life.

There are countless stories in the Bible of people who were ill-equipped to master the tasks at hand.

— Moses was supposed to lead a couple of million Jewish slaves out of Egypt, but he was a stuttering fugitive.

— David was a shepherd boy who killed a giant with a rock.

— Gideon was hiding in a hole when God told him he was going to defeat an enemy army.

— A virgin teenager was told by an angel she was going to have God's son. Talk about insufficient tools!

Whatever you face today, whatever has you stymied or discouraged, prayerfully consider the tools needed to change your life and then go after them. Don't assume you are too awful or too uneducated or too…whatever. All you lack are the tools to live your best life. As for me, I can't do life, don't want to do life, without God, so I would recommend Him to you.

Further Reading

For Moses's story: Exodus 1-15

For David's: 1 Samuel 17

For Gideon's: Judges 6

For Mary's: Luke 1:26-38

Philippians 4:9 *And this same God who takes care of me will supply all your needs from his glorious riches, which have been given to us in Christ Jesus.*

James 1:5 *If you need wisdom, ask our generous God, and he will give it to you. He will not rebuke you for asking.*

Philippians 2:13 *For God is working in you, giving you the desire and the power to do what pleases him.*

Ephesians 3:20 *Now all glory to God, who is able, through his mighty power at work within us, to accomplish infinitely more than we might ask or think.*

[Marriage, Perseverance, Transformation, Trust]

Chapter 10

A Snapshot of....

SACRED FRIES

A young woman, weak and very ill, sat on the steps of the Eldoret District Hospital in Kenya, Africa. My friend Juli, an American hospice director, sat down beside her and asked, "What can I do for you?" "French fries," the woman said, "I'd like some French fries."

Juli is one of the wisest and most compassionate women I know. The Living Room, the hospice she founded, is nestled in the rolling hills of Kenya, dotted by tiny mud homes, cattle, cornfields and too much poverty. Juli and her staff work to provide freedom from pain, shame, and isolation for those who are gravely ill. Juli told me the story of finding this young woman on the stairs of that hospital, dying of AIDS, and her unexpected request. If you're like me, you're thinking, "French fries?" She needs medicine or water or a bed. But Juli helped the frail woman into the hospital cafeteria where she ordered French fries.

Was it a magical moment? Did she suddenly begin to feel better? Sadly, no. The young woman died soon after this encounter. The point? Those simple fries were sacred—consecrated and holy because of the gift of time, attention, and love offered. In that young woman's final hours, she was seen, she was known, she was touched by the love of another and by the love of God. Even deep-fried potato strips become sacred when given with love and compassion.

In my busyness and distraction, I wonder how many people I blow past without even noticing. And if I do notice, how often do I stop, see, ask and act? I'm not suggesting that every person we see is our assignment, but are we even aware of others' needs around us? Are we even looking with eyes that care? We are each a part of this beautiful mess called humanity. We can see people as miserable, broken and worthless, or we can see them as living souls doing their best. Yes, there are evil people, but most of us are just beautiful messes making our way through life. I am deeply and sadly aware of how many opportunities I have passed up to offer a sacred gift to a friend or stranger: a smile, a touch, a listening ear, a small plate of fries.

Something isn't sacred because it is expensive or a heroic endeavor. Acts of kindness or tangible gifts become sacred when they are offered without obligation or recognition, and given in the name of love, grace, and Jesus. Generous kindness matters. It always matters.

I have been touched by the sacred. Several years ago, a friend of mine gave me a gift certificate for a facial, my first! She paid for it beforehand, including a tip, then met me at the salon and told her esthetician exactly what I needed. I felt very cared for (and to be honest, a bit anxious). After a truly amazing experience, the esthetician also offered to do my eyebrows. As she plucked and shaped and trimmed (apparently, I had a caterpillar growing up there), I had tears rolling into my ears. She kept stopping and asking if she was hurting me. "No, I'm fine." But the tears wouldn't stop. I finally choked out that I was overwhelmed by her kindness. She didn't have to do this for me. I had done nothing to deserve it and she wasn't getting paid extra for it. It was one human being showing kindness to another—a frazzled young woman struggling in her marriage and raising two small children. She blessed me so thoroughly that today, some thirty-plus years later, I can still remember the feeling of her hands on my face, the kindness of her smile, the softness of her voice, and the sacredness of the gift she gave me.

There is a story Jesus tells in the gospel of Luke about a man who was beaten up, robbed and left for dead on the side of the road. Two religious types came by and sidestepped the man lying there. A third man, not a religious leader, took care of the man, got him to an inn and covered all his expenses. The care the beaten man received was sacred and holy, for it was done in love. (Luke 10: 25-37)

Several years ago, my mom, in her late 80s, was in a grocery store and saw "a tiny older woman" trying to reach something on a higher shelf. Mom, at 5'9", asked, "May I help you with that?" The woman was so grateful she had tears in her eyes. It was neither difficult nor expensive but it was a holy moment because Mom saw her and cared.

Giving a sacred gift is really that easy. Keep your eyes and heart open, choose to offer your gift and serve another person with time, attention, service or resources. Think about it! You can do something holy today. How cool is that?

Further Reading

Isaiah 58:10 *Feed the hungry and help those in trouble. Then your light will shine out from the darkness, and the darkness around you will be as bright as noon.*

Galatians 6:2 *Share each other's burdens, and in this way obey the law of Christ.*

Matthew 10:40-42 *"We are intimately linked in this harvest work. Anyone who accepts what you do, accepts me, the One who sent you. Anyone who accepts what I do accepts my Father, who sent me. Accepting a messenger of God is as good as being God's messenger. Accepting someone's help is as good as giving someone help. This is a large work I've called you into, but don't be overwhelmed by it. It's best to start small. Give a cool cup of water to someone who is thirsty, for instance. The smallest act of giving or receiving makes you a true apprentice. You won't lose out on a thing."*

[Grace, Kindness, Serving]

Chapter 11

A Snapshot of….

A Trustworthy Compass

In the olden days (when I was young) when you asked for directions, you would probably hear something like, "Head north for about an hour until you see the river, then go right for a while until you come to a bridge. Cross it and head east until you come to the town." Obviously, much different than our modern GPS systems: "Proceed three point two miles then turn right. Turn right in point two miles. Turn right. Recalculating."

The main difference is that we used to watch for landmarks and signs that guided us on the next portion of our journey. We knew our ultimate goal, but the journey was a matter of discovery along the way. With GPS we don't even think about it—a robot could do what we do. And if you use Waze or Google Maps, you're even directed around slowed traffic, so you don't have to think about where you're going, you just let the app guide you.

I believe life should be more about the journey than just the destination. What we do every day and how we do it is an ongoing discovery of the people, events, and places we encounter. With the pace of Southern California life and my pattern of just getting to my destination, I am on autopilot most of the time. Even when I take a walk, I usually have my earbuds in and am somewhere else in a podcast or story, not really present to the surrounding trees, flowers, and just…life. I'm trying to change this pattern but apparently it is fairly ingrained in me.

This is not a snapshot of profound revelation. It isn't a new idea, I know. But as I look at this simple compass, I am reminded to "head north" and keep my eyes, my mind, and my heart open to all that is before me, to see both the beauty and the need. By doing so, I will see nature and people in real time. And if my heart is in the right place, I will find countless ways to show love and care for the people I encounter. I can make a difference. It doesn't have to be huge; even the smallest thing done in love can make a big difference to someone else.

I recently heard a dear friend tell of coming upon a stalled car on a freeway off-ramp. Cars had to navigate around both sides of the stalled car to get on their way. Traffic was backing up quickly even onto the freeway. My friend pulled over and got out to help. As he did, he saw several others do the same. In just moments, they had pushed the car to safety off the ramp and traffic could proceed freely. I wonder how many cars had squeezed by, not acknowledging the situation other than to be irritated. Gratefully, there were enough who chose to see, care, and act. It was only minutes, but it made a huge impact on the driver of that car and the many people caught in the backup.

Luke 10:25-37 tells the story of a man who had been beaten, robbed, and left for dead. Several people walked by, even crossing the road to avoid having to walk past the bloodied man lying there. But one man, just one man, saw, cared, and acted. We call him the Good Samaritan. For him, the journey was as important as the destination. If I am ever in trouble, I pray that there is someone like him who comes my way.

I am trying to slow down and intentionally be present on my daily journey through life. Whether I leave the house or not, am I present to my surroundings and the people in my life? Are we aware of the goodness that makes up our home, family, and friends? Are you grateful for the work you do that provides for you? Consider this a reminder to be aware of the journey, to stop and smell the roses, and to help others do the same when you can.

Further Reading

Read the story of the Good Samaritan in Luke 10:25-37

Proverbs 11:25 *"The one who blesses others is abundantly blessed; those who help others are helped."*

Luke 6:37-38 MSG *"Don't pick on people, jump on their failures, criticize their faults—unless, of course, you want the same* *treatment. Don't condemn those who are down; that hardness can boomerang. Be easy on people; you'll find life a lot easier. Give away your life; you'll find life given back, but not merely given back—given back with bonus and blessing. Giving, not getting, is the way. Generosity begets generosity."*

John 15:12 *"I've told you these things for a purpose: that my joy might be your joy, and your joy wholly mature. This is my command: Love one another the way I loved you. This is the very best way to love. Put your life on the line for your friends. You are my friends when you do the things I command you. I'm no longer calling you servants because servants don't understand what their master is thinking and planning. No, I've named you friends because I've let you in on everything I've heard from the Father."*

[Faith, Guidance, Serving]

Chapter 12

A Snapshot of....

BLINDING FOG

An entry from my personal journal on July 11, 2010:

> *A day shrouded in fog...that's what it feels like today. Buddy died yesterday and today I have to talk with the mortuary people and decide what to do with his body...talk with Pic about doing a memorial service...it's a day that I cannot see what will happen or even what I should do. I am numb and lost. And so I take Your hand as I face this day shrouded in fog. You see clearly...I see very, very little. I trust You...I rely on You...I need you desperately. Take my hand, Father. You know the way.*

I love the mountains. Living in Southern California provides me the opportunity to easily drive up to them for a getaway in about an hour. There is something so fresh and clean about being in the mountains. I'm not hesitant to drive up winding roads and the drive is beautiful. Unless there is fog. *Oy vey*. Fog.

It's not uncommon to be on my way to a mountain cabin and suddenly drive into a wall of fog where I can only see fifteen feet ahead of me on a road that winds and curves crazily, and plummets hundreds of feet just to my right. It is scary, not invigorating. I've learned to go as slow as I need to and as carefully as I want to. The great blessing is that sometimes a truck will come up behind me, pass me, then slow down so I can see his taillights. It is an invitation to follow him. He knows the road; it is familiar to him. Suddenly I feel my white-knuckle grip on the steering wheel loosen and my shoulders relax a bit. Someone who knows the way is leading me.

There is so much of life that feels like fog. Whether it is difficult seasons, circumstances, or fear, we sometimes face life unable to see or discern exactly what to do, where to go or how to get there. Sometimes the fog is a big decision like marriage, a job offer, or finances. Or it can be a crisis like a death, loss of job or severe health issues. It might also be a dream that compels us forward, but we fear going after it or don't know how to begin. Fog can spring up at any time in life; you've likely faced it several times. How can we best respond to it?

Slow down. Don't keep barreling forward when you aren't sure where you're going. I have had the privilege (and pain) of being invited into troubled, broken marriages. It may be infidelity or other betrayal, or it might simply be that pain and brokenness over time have chipped away at anything that binds two people together. My first piece of advice is often, "Until you know what to do, don't do anything." That may sound overly-simplistic, but I've found that when big decisions are made out of intense emotion it can lead to regret. This is the fog effect. You might ultimately make the same decision, but you've thought about it with reasoning and input. When you find yourself suddenly in dense fog, do you hit the gas and speed up? Do you slam on the brakes? Hopefully not, that's dangerous! But slow down? Yes.

Process your situation. If you're a praying person, that's the optimal place to begin. (If you're not, may I suggest that's a good time to start? Just sayin'.) Processing your situation means that you play out possibilities in your mind and consider alternative responses before acting. Talk with trusted friends who are as likely to challenge your thinking as to encourage it. If you are thinking of leaving your spouse, don't talk to your marriage-hating friend. If you are considering a big job offer, don't talk to a friend who can't hold a job. Choose a friend or mentor who knows the road and can see through the fog better than you can, like my nameless friend in the truck. Process before you make a decision.

Act. Once you have slowed down and processed with trusted people, then make your move. Stir up your courage and do what you need to do. While it was great that the truck driver pulled in front of me to help me navigate the foggy mountain road, it would have done me no good unless I followed him. I chose to trust and keep driving to my destination. Your action may be a difficult conversation or a big life move. Don't set up camp in the fog and let it define the quality and freedom of your life. Fog happens. It doesn't own you.

My husband Budd died suddenly in the wee hours of a Saturday morning. It was unexpected and final. There was no preparation or planning. The fog was intense—there was so much I didn't know. I had three important resources in my life: God, my family, and my friends. They were the caravan of trucks that pulled in front of me in the blinding fog and led the way for me. My sisters flew to LA, and my son, daughter and daughter-in-law, in their own grief, walked with me every step of the way through decisions, paperwork and a new way of living. My church family handled the memorial service, food, prayers…so much. And through it all, there was God—His tangible presence as I cried and His strength to hold me up through those first few weeks and beyond. I never want to do fog alone. If you don't have anyone in your life today that you know would walk through fog with you, I encourage you to begin nurturing those kinds of relationships—with God, with family if you can, and with friends. We were never meant to navigate this life alone.

I pray that your days of fog will be few and that your resources will be mighty.

Further Reading

Psalm 23:2 *He lets me rest in green meadows; he leads me beside peaceful streams.*

Psalm 48:14 *For that is what God is like. He is our God forever and ever, and he will guide us until we die.*

Isaiah 30:21 *Your own ears will hear him. Right behind you a voice will say, "This is the way you should go," whether to the right or to the left.*

Isaiah 42:16 *I will lead blind Israel down a new path, guiding them along an unfamiliar way. I will brighten the darkness before them and smooth out the road ahead of them. Yes, I will indeed do these things; I will not forsake them.*

Psalm 25:5 *Lead me by your truth and teach me, for you are the God who saves me. All day long I put my hope in you.*

[Choices, Grief, Guidance, Wisdom]

Chapter 13

A Snapshot of....

CAUTION: FINES DOUBLED

Yellow road signs are cautionary, warning drivers to be on alert: "Men at Work," "Yield," "Reduced Speed Ahead." Paying attention in these areas is critical for your safety and others'. One such important caution is "Fines Doubled in Construction Zones." If a speeding ticket would normally cost you $100, this one is going to be $200 (yes, I'm a math whiz). Imagine how important this caution is when applied to our daily life.

There is maturing and change that happens at every age, times when we are essentially "under construction." We face circumstances and people that require us to think, compromise, problem-solve and sacrifice. Along the way, we also learn to love and be loved. These life construction zones are the seasons when we are given opportunities to become our better selves. As in driving, we have the option to pay attention or to ignore. Whether marriage, money, job opportunities, sickness, or loss, we choose to learn and grow or we ignore all of the warning signs and make costly mistakes to our own growth or to others.

If, for example, you have over-shopped your budget, you can either learn to live within your means or just get another credit card to absorb the debt. If you choose the latter, you will end up back in that construction zone with the lesson still to be learned. If, however, you begin to live within your financial means, you will one day find that you are out of major debt and free of financial anxiety. The same holds true for construction zones in relationships, self-care, work situations, friendships, etc. When things seem a bit 'torn up' in your life, go after solutions that heal and mend, not that cover up—not just the quick fix.

I am embarrassed to admit that I have actually tried to make a deal with God that goes something like this: "If I wake up skinny, I promise to stay that way." The response I heard almost audibly went something like this: "How about stop eating so much?" I've lived a long time in the construction zone of food addiction. I am learning.

Consider these points about God and our construction zones.

— First, we often question God's intent. We expect His goal for us to be the same as our immediate goals: get answers to all of our questions, experience total comfort, have our needs met, our 'wannas' satisfied, and end our sadness and confusion. Basically, our goal is a cleaner, nicer, happier *us.* But God's ultimate goal is to have us shaped into His image, so that we look and act like the One who made us. That's our best life. That kind of transformation doesn't usually come easily, but it's worth it.

— Secondly, we question God's dependability. While we may start out with a sense of trust or commitment to whatever He directs, we begin to doubt Him when he doesn't act fast enough or in the way we want. Trust Him, He knows what He's doing.

— Finally, we question God's kindness or compassion. Sometimes it is God's very kindness that teaches us patience and trust. It is His mercy and goodness that is shaping the heart of Christ in us. We don't mind having patience, but hurry up already!

We will never be without challenges and opportunities for growth. At my age, I often think, "Enough already! I'm old. I don't want to grow anymore!" But alas, I do. I want my life to matter—to God, to me, to my people and to my little corner of the world. That is only possible as I choose to see obstacles and challenging issues in my life as invitations to grow and change. Lord, help me.

Whatever you're going through or have already gone through, I encourage you to seek new solutions, new habits, better answers, and a fuller life. The consequences (fines) of our difficult seasons (construction zones) don't have to be doubled, tripled, and multiplied. We are amazing, capable people with resources, even if yet undiscovered. Don't wait, don't dodge, and don't neglect. Life will continue to hand us tough seasons, but we don't have to pay double fines.

Further Reading

Exodus 24 through 32 The people of Israel had been freed from slavery and were headed to freedom! God didn't act quickly enough or in the way they wanted. It didn't turn out well. You've maybe seen the movie…now read the book.

2 Kings 7 Even when we are living out the consequences of our own choices or actions, God still works on our behalf if we respond to what He's doing. Read the great story of the Aramean army.

Psalm 121

I look up to the mountains—
does my help come from there?
My help comes from the LORD,
who made the heavens and the earth!
He will not let you stumble and fall;
the one who watches over you will not sleep.
Indeed, he who watches over Israel
never tires and never sleeps.
The LORD himself watches over you!
The LORD stands beside you as your protective shade.
The sun will not hurt you by day,
nor the moon at night.
The LORD keeps you from all evil
and preserves your life.
The LORD keeps watch over you as you come and go,
both now and forever.

Ps 40:17
As for me, I am poor and needy,
but the Lord is thinking about me right now.
You are my helper and my savior.

[Choices, Courage, Pain, Trust]

Chapter 14

A Snapshot of….

A Piano Recital

She is seven and this is her first piano recital. She sits alone on the piano bench, unmoving, as tears slide down her cheeks. She looks out at her parents as if to say, "I can't do it." Her dad, a world class musician, quietly walks up and simply sits beside her as she plays. He could play the piece much better than she does, but that's neither his goal nor his purpose. The playing is hers; he only sits close to let her know she is not alone and she can do it. When it is over, she is filled with satisfaction and pride. She did it. She may not even be aware of how much her father's simple presence gave her the courage she needed.

This little analogy illustrates how, so often in life, we face great challenges that feel beyond our ability or courage. We hesitate to even try, yet we know we must. But how? God promises to always be near, to be present with us at all times. We may not feel Him, but He is there, and His presence alone can give us the courage and fortitude to keep going.

Family and friends have stood by me in difficult times and "sat on the piano bench." When Budd died suddenly, my sisters flew here immediately and just stayed close; my friends handled innumerable details. My kids, though living their own grief, walked with me in the difficult months following our loss. God has always been present, and often uses people to sit on my piano bench on His behalf.

I look back at the countless times I have been faced with big decisions and big opportunities. Whether it's being invited to teach in Australia, asked to come on staff at my church, or deciding to do graduate studies, left to my own limitations, I flounder. But God has always been close and provided people to walk alongside and encourage me. I could not have done any of those things on my own. And this makes me wonder, is there someone I could help by sitting on their piano bench?

Jesus didn't just call a group of guys and tell them to go teach people about Him. He lived with, walked with, taught and encouraged them, just as He does with us today. The apostle Paul believed in a young man named Timothy who became his mission partner and ultimately led a fledgling church. Paul sat on Timothy's piano bench.

Whether it is through a person or an awareness of God's presence, we do not have to face the stuff of life alone. It feels that way sometimes but there is another way. God promises to be close and to give us what we need in life. Are you open to that? Do you allow others into your circumstances so that they can help and encourage you? And are you open to being present and with someone facing a hard season of life? If not, it's time to make a change.

God promises us His Holy Spirit as a teacher, comforter, and guide. We don't ever need to sit on the piano bench alone. It's not about who can do it best, it's about us doing our best at what we're created and called to be. Take heart. You don't have to be alone on the stage of life.

Further Reading

Isaiah 43:2 *When you go through deep waters, I will be with you. When you go through rivers of difficulty, you will not drown. When you walk through the fire of oppression, you will not be burned up; the flames will not consume you.*

Isaiah 41:10 *Don't be afraid, for I am with you. Don't be discouraged, for I am your God. I will strengthen you and help you. I will hold you up with my victorious right hand.*

Isaiah 41:13 *For I hold you by your right hand— I, the LORD your God. And I say to you, 'Don't be afraid. I am here to help you.'*

Matthew 28:19,20 *'Therefore, go and make disciples of all the nations, baptizing them in the name of the Father and the Son and the Holy Spirit. Teach these new disciples to obey all the commands I have given you. And be sure of this: I am with you always, even to the end of the age.'*

John 14:27 *I am leaving you with a gift—peace of mind and heart. And the peace I give is a gift the world cannot give. So don't be troubled or afraid.*

1 Timothy 1:1,2 *This letter is from Paul, an apostle of Christ Jesus, appointed by the command of God our Savior and Christ Jesus, who gives us hope. I am writing to Timothy, my true son in the faith. May God the Father and Christ Jesus our Lord give you grace, mercy, and peace.*

[Encouragement, Presence, Relationships, Support]

Chapter 15

A Snapshot of....

Rainbows and Cement

She sat down across from me in my office. I knew her and her family as part of my church. Married with two young children, she had come for counseling, or so she said. She had met a man, a father at her kids' school, and they were in love. "God brought us together." I listened quietly and let her tell her story. When she was finished, I simply asked, "What is it you want from me?" Her reply was clear: "I don't want your opinion. I just wanted you to know what I'm going to do." Two families were blown up because these two people "fell in love."

Over my years of pastoral counseling, I have heard countless stories from men and women, wives and husbands, who were no longer "in love" and wanted me to guide them out of their marriage with my blessing, or God's blessing. One woman cited "emotional abandonment." One man complained that his wife and daughter complicated his career as a musician. One young wife said her husband didn't feel "emotionally safe" for her because he didn't understand her. A variety of reasons for a common malady: we don't really know what love is.

We usually think of love as rainbows, butterflies, and sunsets. A wonderful feeling and a fluttering heart, daydreams and possibilities. Our culture—movies, books, music, television, and social media—has taught us this very thing and we have bought into it completely. I was married for thirty-nine years, and I can assure you that neither Budd nor I spent every day with our hearts aflutter and goofy grins on our faces. If love is no more than a warm feeling, we are all doomed. That feeling is not sustainable.

Real love is an attitude, a commitment, and a covenant. Love is more like cement than rainbows. When guarded, protected, and nurtured, love becomes a foundation upon which to build a life. Unlike a rainbow, real love does not dissipate when life gets difficult and hearts feel dry. Infatuation, crushes, and daydreams are not the stuff upon which to build a life. They feel wonderful but they are not permanent. This is not just about marriage, either. The way we love our friends and our families also requires commitment, honesty and sometimes, sheer grit. But that's what love does.*

So, how in the world do we love like that? The Bible gives a clear picture of God's love and the love we can experience and share in First Corinthians where it says:

> *Love is patient and kind. Love is not jealous or boastful or proud or rude. It does not demand its own way. It is not irritable, and it keeps no record of being wronged. It does not rejoice about injustice but rejoices whenever the truth wins out. Love never gives up, never loses faith, is always hopeful, and endures through every circumstance.* (13: 4-7)

Obviously, neither I nor anyone else I know love perfectly. Just the idea of "keeps no record of wrongs" is a mighty challenge for me. Apparently, I have a great memory, at least in areas where I've been hurt or offended. The point is that as I read the list above, I am drawn to be the kind of person who can love my family, friends, and even strangers with a patient, kind, thoughtful, persistent, and hopeful love. And the deep longing of my heart is that the people who care about me have those characteristics in massive supply. I need that kind of love desperately.

If God only loved us with feelings, we would be in deep trouble. His love is intentional and active. My only hope of ever loving and being loved this way is through God. He not only loves me, but daily teaches me to love the way He does. I know the people who love me have been given to me as gifts. Their love heals, helps and presses me to be my best self.

If you are personally acquainted with God, I encourage you to tell Him, right now, that you're grateful for His love in you and through you. Thank Him for the people who come to mind as you think about being loved. If you don't feel connected to God enough to do that, I encourage you to just think about Him. Allow a little space in your thoughts to accept that you are unbelievably loved by Him. Let His love enter your heart and mind with healing and hope. His love truly is cement and it's more than enough to build your entire life on.

> *I know there are situations of safety, abuse, and abandonment that can ruin relationships. I have lived them. Not every situation can be endured in the hope it will change. If that is your situation, I encourage you to get help. In this snapshot I'm talking about relationships that are discarded because we don't "feel" a certain way toward someone we're committed to in a relationship.

Further Reading

Philippians 1:3 *Every time I think of you, I give thanks to my God.*

Proverbs 17:17 *A friend is always loyal, and a brother is born to help in time of need.* (This includes sisters, BTW!)

Ecclesiastes 4:9-10 *Two people are better off than one, for they can help each other succeed. If one person falls, the other can reach out and help. But someone who falls alone is in real trouble.*

Jeremiah 31:3 *Long ago the LORD said to His people: "I have loved you, my people, with an everlasting love. With unfailing love I have drawn you to myself."* (God spoke this to His chosen people who continually rejected and disobeyed Him. That is concrete love.)

Isaiah 54:10 *"For the mountains may move and the hills disappear, but even then my faithful love for you will remain. My covenant of blessing will never be broken," says the* Lord, *who has mercy on you."*

Galatians 5:22-23 *But the Holy Spirit produces this kind of fruit in our lives: love, joy, peace, patience, kindness, goodness, faithfulness, gentleness, and self-control. There is no law against these things!* (If you struggle to love others as you want to, we are promised the very things we need through God's Spirit in those who believe Him. This is healing and sustaining love.)

[Choices, Love, Marriage, Relationships]

Chapter 16

A Snapshot of....

Red Mary Janes

I stood in a small circle of third-grade girlfriends laughing and talking (probably about boys). I can still remember the incredible feeling of belonging; that is, until I glanced down at our feet and suddenly something inside me froze. I actually didn't belong. It was obvious. Four pairs of shoes looked cute, girly, and relatively clean. My shoes were cast-offs given to the "poor family." A wave of such sadness, shame, and aloneness washed over me I can still feel it today.

I wonder sometimes if that's why I have thirty pairs of shoes today (I just went into my closet and counted). Granted, most of them are quite casual, but I have options no matter what I'm wearing. To be honest, I don't think about shoes all the time anymore, though I used to. Why? Because somehow my identity got mixed up with my shoes. I never wanted to have the worst shoes in the circle again (though I don't think I consciously saw the connection until later in life). Several years ago, for my birthday, my husband bought me a small pair of red ceramic Mary Janes, the epitome of little girl shoes. He knew my story and wanted to reframe it, an incredibly loving act on his part.

I'm certain other experiences have shaped my identity, most of which I'm not fully aware. But one thing is certain: I do not have to live in a broken identity shaped by my past. Neither poverty, alcoholism, abuse, or any of the dark tentacles of childhood need define me any longer. I choose to establish who I can be, who I am. It doesn't come without work—and often the help of others—but it is well worth the investment of time, tears, and effort. I am what I am and that's all that I am (to quote Popeye, the Sailor Man).

I am no longer the sum total of my most broken parts. I am not perfect (far, far from it), nor am I the victim of my circumstances. I am in the process of becoming more whole and free than ever before. Again, that process is worth the time and effort.

If you are a person of faith, you are promised a new identity. I am a child of God, adopted by a perfect, loving Father who has given me His name, identity, and legacy. I am not limited by my past but am becoming more the person I desire to be. That is my place of peace and hope.

Even if you are not a person of faith, don't remain stuck in the messages from your past that say you are not enough or you are too broken for hope. Choose to share your life with people who believe in you, regardless of the shoes you wear. Being known, accepted, and loved is good for us. I am convinced, though, that only the love of God can heal our deepest wounds. And He wants to.

Further Reading

Eph 2:10 *For we are God's masterpiece. He has created us anew in Christ Jesus, so we can do the good things he planned for us long ago.*

Jeremiah 31:3 *Long ago the LORD said to Israel: "I have loved you, my people, with an everlasting love. With unfailing love I have drawn you to myself."*

Isaiah 43:1 *But now, O Jacob, listen to the LORD who created you. O Israel, the one who formed you says, "Do not be afraid, for I have ransomed you. I have called you by name; you are mine."*

1 John 3:1 *See how very much our Father loves us, for he calls us his children, and that is what we are!*

[Faith, Identity, Relationships]

Chapter 17

A Snapshot of....

FORGOTTEN POM-POMS

Pom-poms are standard factory issue on all human beings. We are created to celebrate and encourage other people, and to be celebrated and encouraged ourselves. One of the first things we teach babies to do is clap their hands. I have held the chubby little hands of my kids and my grandkids as I chanted, "patty-cake, patty-cake...." When these little ones do something extraordinary like putting a cookie in their mouth, we applaud wildly. When they count to ten, recite their ABC's, and tie their own shoes we go wild with praise. Potty-training is rewarded with the likes of an Olympic Gold Medal. We are made for praise. We are made to praise.

For most of us, it seems that growing up has been a systematic lesson in subduing our pom-poms. School grades seem to focus on what we're not good at rather than the areas we excel. "Good job!" is the response when a kid does something well, but when that same child does something wrong the response is much stronger, carrying heavy consequences. Somehow, we learn to mildly accept our successes yet focus on our shortcomings, and we do the same to others.

This is not a study on child-rearing or acceptable means of discipline, but a call to the revival of pom-poms. Seriously. Go to the attic or the garage and dig out those pom-poms (metaphorically speaking). Pause for a few minutes and ponder the question, *What have I done well today?* Perhaps you went to work, did your job, came home and hung out with friends or family. Nothing special? Wait! You went to your job and gave a day's work for a day's wage. That's faithfulness. Shake those pom-poms! Were you home today working, schooling your kids, planning dinner and straightening the house? Get out those pom-poms! You have served your family well today, with your investment of time and energy. Perhaps you went to the beach or hiked the foothills or read a book. Well done! God's creation, solitude, and self-care are all worthy of celebration. Flap those pom-poms! I trust you are getting the idea here. Recognize what is worth celebrating and where in your life you are living faithfully.

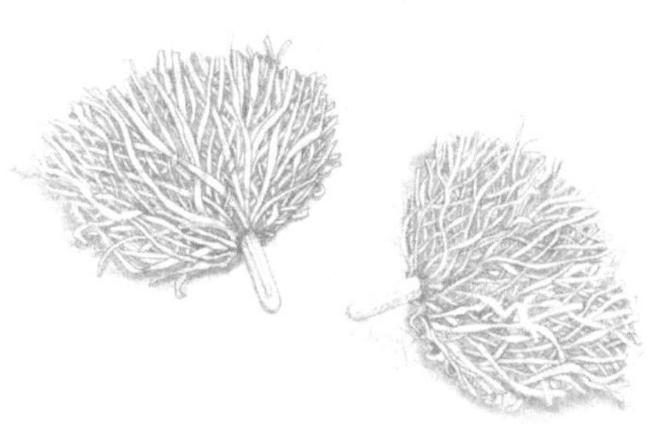

How about with others? Where do you see your spouse or roommate living well and faithfully? Is there a coworker who is putting in a lot of effort or has helped you out? Have you really praised your kids today? I'm not talking about flattery or making things up. I'm talking about having eyes to see the good in ourselves and in others. It doesn't take something monumental to deserve celebration and encouragement, it just takes someone noticing when there is faithfulness, dependability, and joy. If you're at the market and the checker is particularly kind, whip out those pom-poms and make their day. Sometimes a sincere smile at someone is a beautiful pom-pom experience.

Here's the thing, once you retrieve your dusty pom-poms and begin to use them, you will find countless opportunities to encourage, celebrate and delight others as well as yourself. It becomes a lifestyle rather than an event; you become the joy-bringer to those around you. If you deem yourself too dignified for pom-poms, then I'm sorry for you. You will miss out on so many chances for your heart to expand and your life to be lit up. Pom-poms are standard factory issue for each one of us; with a little practice, you can perfect the use of them.

Further Reading

Ephesians 4:29 *Let no evil talk come out of your mouths, but only what is useful for building up, as there is need, so that your words may give grace to those who hear.*

Colossians 4:6 *Let your speech always be gracious, seasoned with salt, so that you may know how you ought to answer everyone.*

Proverbs 16:24 *Pleasant words are like a honeycomb, sweetness to the soul and health to the body.*

Proverbs 25:11 *A word fitly spoken is like apples of gold in a setting of silver.*

Isaiah 50:4 *The Lord GOD has given me the tongue of a teacher, that I may know how to sustain the weary with a word. Morning by morning he wakens my ear to listen as those who are taught.*

Matthew 25:4 *His master said to him, 'Well done, good and trustworthy servant; you have been trustworthy in a few things, I will put you in charge of many things; enter into the joy of your master.'*

[Encouragement, Faithfulness, Relationships]

Chapter 18

A Snapshot of....

A GARBAGE BARGE

Forgiveness is a challenge (understatement of the year). During a particular season of my life where I was struggling with events in my past, I realized how the brokenness of my childhood caused me to carry into adulthood a lot of shame, distrust and bitterness—not great qualities on which to build a healthy and fulfilling life.

As I wrestled with the incredibly negative effects of these feelings a picture came to mind: I was standing on a sidewalk that ran along a canal. Floating in the canal was a barge covered with garbage, human waste, rotten food, and all manner of refuse. It was so putrid that steam rose from it. A large nautical rope was tied to the barge, with the other end tied around my neck. I could walk up and down the canal, in essence, pulling the putrid barge behind, which gave a false sense of freedom. But I could not walk away from the barge. So, I purposed to clean it up; I promised I would. I felt God gently tell me that I could not clean it up, I needed to take the rope from around my neck.

What seemed a logical and simple piece of advice was very difficult for me. The barge was my stuff—wrong things done against me and wrong things I had done—my identity, really. Finally, though, I carefully pulled the noose from around my neck and slowly walked away across the green rolling hills ahead of me. I made the decision to forgive my grandfather for the abuse, to allow God's grace to handle my shame, brokenness, and sin, and to believe that I could walk in freedom.

Forgiveness is letting go of the right to pay back for hurt done to me. Forgiveness can feel like proclaiming that the offense was not a big deal or that the offender should get off the hook. Nothing in that feels like justice, and that is not how God works. When we forgive, we pass the offense into His capable hands—the perfect balance of justice and mercy. Whatever the situation, be it an intentional harmful offense like abuse or a slight to my fragile ego, forgiveness is the only option that results in wholeness and freedom.

It has been my experience that forgiveness can be understood as a three-stage process: God's forgiveness of us, our acceptance of that forgiveness, and our extending forgiveness to others. It seems to me that any shortcuts or editing of this process can cripple us and get us stuck.

The Bible tells us the very first people were a couple named Adam and Eve. They hung out with God in a perfect garden. God told them they could have *anything* in the garden except this *one* tree. So, like us, they picked a ripe ol' apple or orange or kumquat from the "forbidden tree" and ate it. God told the nation of Israel not to worship any other god but Him or there'd be judgment. And yet they made idols to worship. God told, God told, God told, and people did it anyway.

But God never gave up on His prized creation: people. From animal skins to animal sacrifices, He always made a way to be in relationship with broken people. Ultimately, God's immense love for people brought Him to a cross outside Jerusalem. Forgiveness was a necessity if there was to be relationship, and forgiveness had to be more than God winking at or ignoring sin. God's offer of forgiveness to us came at a great price: God became human, a man named Jesus who took upon Himself the guilt of every sin you or I have ever committed, or will ever commit. He chose to bear the weight and penalty of all sin so that forgiveness, freedom, and eternal life might be offered to humankind, to us.

Forgiveness is a gift offered and we are asked to receive it. Let's say I were to offer you a check for a million dollars (don't get excited...purely hypothetical). The check is made out in your name, signed by me, and backed by the funds to make it valid. I could stand there with the check in hand extended to you, but if you don't take it, you will never enjoy the benefits of the money. This is a picture of forgiveness. God extends forgiveness to us because of Jesus. The check, as it were, is made out to us and signed by God, with all of the resources to make it valid. What we do in response to that offer determines whether or not we will enjoy all of the benefits of this extreme forgiveness and the life and freedom that result. He takes the rope from around our neck and removes the barge.

The final stage of forgiveness comes with the challenge for us to forgive others. Without receiving forgiveness from God, I don't think I can forgive myself or anyone else. If I feel responsible and accountable for every wrong I've committed, then I will certainly expect others to own their guilt and offenses, too. It's a terrible cycle, isn't it? But it works both ways. I have found that my willingness (even if it's hesitant) to forgive others helps me continue to grow in forgiveness toward myself, and I am desperately in need of that ongoing strength to live in freedom from guilt and shame.

Whatever you're carrying against others, yourself, or God, let it go. Forgive. Unforgiveness gives an offender the ability to hurt and control your life even years after the offense. My grandfather died when I was seventeen, but I didn't choose to forgive him until I was in my thirties. I regret giving him the power to intrude on my marriage and my happiness. Is there someone you need to forgive? Is there someone from whom you should ask forgiveness? It's a great day to clear the air in your life. Take the rope from your neck and walk free. You are worth it, truly.

It has been a process to walk in forgiveness and grace but I have never gone back to the canal, or to what it represents. I may not know how to live fully in freedom but I'm learning. I pray the same for you.

Further Reading

Psalm 86:5 *O Lord, you are so good, so ready to forgive, so full of unfailing love for all who ask for your help.*

Colossians 3:12-13 *Since God chose you to be the holy people he loves, you must clothe yourselves with tenderhearted mercy, kindness, humility, gentleness and patience. Make allowance for each other's faults and forgive anyone who offends you. Remember, the Lord forgave you so you must forgive others.*

Ephesians 1:7 *He is so rich in kindness and grace that he purchased our freedom with the blood of his Son and forgave our sins.*

Ephesians 4:32 *Instead, be kind to each other, tenderhearted, forgiving one another, just as God through Christ has forgiven you.*

Matthew 5:23-24 *So if you are presenting a sacrifice at the altar in the Temple and you suddenly remember that someone has something against you, leave your sacrifice there at the altar. Go and be reconciled to that person. Then come and offer your sacrifice.*

Matthew 6:9-13 *Pray like this: Our Father in heaven, may your name be kept holy. May your Kingdom come soon. May your will be done on earth, as it is in heaven. Give us today the food we need, and forgive us our sins, as we have forgiven those* *who sin against us. And don't let us yield to temptation, but rescue us from the evil one.*

[Despair, Forgiveness, Freedom, Grace]

Chapter 19

A Snapshot of....

BETTER TOGETHER

One day, late in the afternoon when Matt was five and Anna was two, I asked Matt to take Anna and straighten up their room. Matt was a very responsible five-year-old and liked to organize things (traits he still has today). As I prepared dinner, I paid little attention to them for a while because there were no sounds of conflict or disaster coming from their room.

Standing at the sink washing vegetables, I heard my dear boy's trembling voice behind me say, "Mommy...I can't do it." I turned and there stood Matty with giant tears rolling down his cheeks. "I'm sorry, Mommy, I can't do it." My first thought was to be alarmed that something had happened to Anna, but she stood behind him in two-year-old oblivion grinning at me.

"What can't you do, honey? What's wrong?"

"I can't fix it, Mommy, it's too big."

"What's too big, Matty?"

"My room...I can't do it."

More giant tears rolled down his cheeks. I took his hand. "Let's go look, honey."

As we walked into the kids' bedroom, I immediately understood the problem. In his desire to clean the room really well, they had emptied everything into the center of the room: sheets, blankets, pillows, books, puzzles, toys, shoes and clothing. Anything they could reach was now on the floor. It was quite a sight.

I looked down at my son who still held my hand. His tiny shoulders were stooped and a couple more tears escaped his big brown eyes. He just didn't know what to do with the mess he had created. I looked at Anna and she was still grinning at the giant pile, oblivious to what it meant (...ah, to be two again).

I knelt down. "Matty, dinner is about ready so let's go eat. After dinner, Daddy and I will help. It's okay, honey. It will be fine." We ate, cleared the dishes, and the four of us went into their room. In literally ten minutes the room was perfectly ordered and for our son, a great burden had been lifted. It turned out to be a great and even fun time for all of us.

The problem wasn't a big deal to me or Budd. But for our son, it looked insurmountable. We could have played hardball. "You two made the mess, now you clean it up. Figure it out." But we know a five-year-old's limitations (even with the "help" of a two-year-old) and the answer was "us" rather than "them." The principle is still true today. "Us" is better than "me" or "them." Together, life is so much more doable.

Where in your life today could you use some support? What do you find yourself ill-equipped to handle on your own? Maybe it's marriage or parenting, finances, family, or friendships. Perhaps it's depression or physical limitations. Whatever it is you face today, you don't have to face it alone. Look around at what God has provided for you or through you. It may be professionals we engage or friends we open up to. A small thing for you may be huge for someone else, or what seems massive to you may be an easy thing for another person. It happens all the time. We just need to be aware and available. Own up to your gifts and abilities, and own up to your needs. All of us together can create a beautiful picture of love and grace.

A couple months after Budd died, I had a major issue with my house. I don't remember the specifics, but I was at a total loss as to how to fix it. I was still so scattered and numb. A friend connected me with a man in our church who ran his own handyman business. He came to my home, quietly fixed whatever was wrong, refused any compensation and assured me he was happy to do it. It was not a big deal to him, but it was huge to me. To this day, I am deeply grateful for his kindness, his skills, and his generosity toward me.

There was a woman in our church who was dying of cancer, without family. She asked me to help organize her apartment and serve as her medical decision-maker. With friends, we did an amazing job on her apartment, organized her medical and financial needs, and walked with her until she took her final breath. It wasn't difficult, but it was crucial for her.

Sometimes we think that helping and serving others has to be an epic task. "Here, let me part the Red Sea for you," or, "I happen to have a few smooth stones here, I'll slay your giant." Jesus calls us to love with what we have: a cup of cold water or aid to a man who has been robbed and beaten. When Jesus wanted to do "God-sized" miracles like feeding five thousand people with just a boy's lunch or turning water to wine to salvage a wedding celebration, He invited people to help by passing out food or filling water jars. (If you aren't familiar with these inspiring stories, I've given you references in the Further Reading section below.) We are never asked to do miracles or to perform feats that only God can do. But we are invited to do what we can. Do what is in front of you. Use what you have and what you know.

You were never intended to manage life alone. You can make a difference for someone today and perhaps others can make a difference for you. Think about it, ask God. Choose today to be a part of God's grand plan that we all thrive…together.

Further Reading

Exodus 14:5-31 A God-sized miracle where God literally opened up the Red Sea so his people could walk across on dry land. God told Moses to put his stick in the water first, that was his role. God parted the water and they walked across on dry land. Wow.

1 Samuel 17:1-51 Goliath was a giant with a bad attitude. He threatened God's people who were petrified of him. God asked a young shepherd to defeat Goliath with a slingshot and five little stones. David did his part and God saw that the stone hit its mark with fatal consequences.

Matthew 10:42 *And if you give even a cup of cold water to one of the least of my followers, you will surely be rewarded.*

Luke 10:25-37 Jesus tells the story of a man who has been robbed and beaten, several people walk past and do nothing. We are challenged to intervene for the sake of others.

Matthew 14:13-21; Mark 6:30-44; Luke 9:10-17; John 6:1-15 Feeding thousands with one little lunch.

2 Corinthians 8:12 *Whatever you give is acceptable if you give it eagerly. And give according to what you have, not what you don't have.*

[Relationships, Restoration, Serving]

Chapter 20

A Snapshot of....

A Priceless Pearl

My favorite earrings are solitary pearls that my husband bought me years ago in Hawaii. I'm not one who matches my earrings to my clothes every day, I don't have the patience. I wear my pearls ninety-nine percent of the time. They are simple and beautiful, every day.

Pearls are formed when a grain of sand or other intrusive element is introduced into the soft tissue (known as the mantle) of a living shelled mollusk. When speaking of gem quality pearls, this is an oyster. To protect itself from the foreign body, the oyster wraps it in

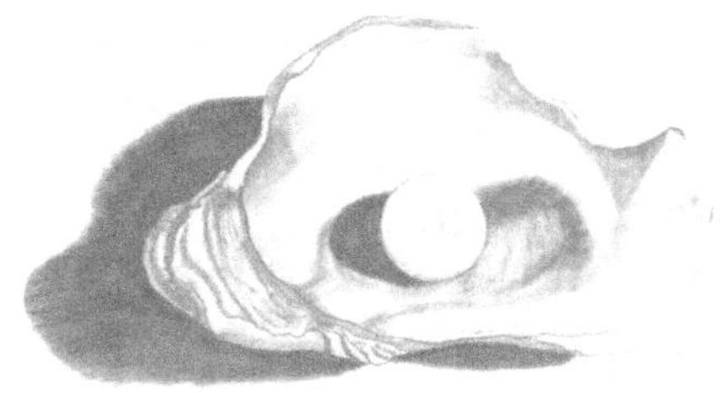

nacre, a substance that seals the intruder and keeps it from harming the oyster. This becomes the pearl and can take up to three years to form. Knowing this makes my little earrings even more precious to me.

During a particularly rough season in my life, I was acutely aware of how constantly irritated and unhappy I was. The picture of a pearl comes to mind when I think of the foreign bodies—disappointments, hurt, unforgiveness—that were wounding my heart in those years. Yet much of what is good in me is a result of those seasons of brokenness, unhappiness, or helplessness that, over time, God used to make something good. Through forgiveness I learned grace, by waiting I learned patience, releasing bitterness taught me kindness, and on it goes.

Too many times, though, we blanket the irritation with bitterness or unforgiveness. This does not create anything of beauty. Rather it remains a place of pain and irritation that festers and robs us of life. The difference is not whether there are irritants affecting our heart and mind, but rather how we deal with them. The nacre the oyster uses to seal the foreign object is a substance natural to the oyster, made of the same stuff as the oyster's shell. We are created in the image of God and thus have access to what we need in order to deal with whatever comes into our lives. It is already a part of us. This is not just about digging deep and coming up with the fortitude to bear it (though we do have to choose to contend for wholeness). Rather, it is about offering these broken places to God, releasing the pain and brokenness, and choosing to live free. God made each of us and has a plan for our lives. He alone can shape pearls out of pain.

Budd and I had some very difficult years in our marriage. It was not about abuse or infidelity, it was about two clueless, broken people attempting one of the most difficult relationship journeys there is. Probably the hardest thing for me to overcome was—wait for it—that he was a *man* and I'm not. I grew up with a single mom and three sisters. I had little context for understanding that men might have different ways of thinking and processing life. Budd and I came from very different family backgrounds. Expectations for the future and pain from the past joined together to trip us up at every turn. My insecurities and lack of trust made it almost impossible for Budd to do anything right or "safe" for me. His typical American family caused him to believe/assume that a wife stayed home, cleaned, cooked, made iced tea every day and greeted him with delight when he arrived home. My single mother worked two jobs and we all pitched in to survive, literally. Budd's expectations felt like demands to me, even his love for me felt like a demand. My independence felt like rejection to Budd. Seriously, people, what's a couple to do?

With counseling and much prayer, Budd and I began to coat the irritation and pain with God's grace, peace, and wisdom. Things began to change, slowly. We began to see small wins. Where my focus for so long had been on our difficult marriage, as we started leaning into grace, forgiveness and acceptance, my focus became no longer Budd but God. The issues (sand) in our marriage did not immediately change, we just began to cover them in grace and acceptance. When Budd passed away a few years ago, I felt such deep gratitude for the years God had restored to us in our marriage.

You won't get through life without pain and suffering, but God has given us the freedom to choose what we will do with the pain that comes to us. You can let it destroy or break you, or you can allow His grace to make something of beauty and value. I was a lazy and slow oyster, but God is incredibly patient and kind. Right now is the very best time to invite Him into your broken places. He really is loving, kind, and powerful. It's worth letting go of the pain.

I will close with the lyrics of a favorite old song by Bill Gaither called *Something Beautiful.*

Something beautiful, something good,
All my confusion he understood.
All I had to offer him was brokenness and strife,
But he made something beautiful out of my life.

This is my story. He has made something beautiful (though not perfect!) out of my life.

Further Reading

Ephesians 2:4-10 *But God is so rich in mercy, and he loved us so much, that even though we were dead because of our sins, he gave us life when he raised Christ from the dead. (It is only by God's grace that you have been saved!) For he raised us from the dead along with Christ and seated us with him in the heavenly realms because we are united with Christ Jesus. So God can point to us in all future ages as examples of the incredible wealth of his grace and kindness toward us, as shown in all he has done for us who are united with Christ Jesus. God saved you by his* *grace when you believed. And you can't take credit for this; it is a gift from God. Salvation is not a reward for the good things we have done, so none of us can boast about it. For we are God's masterpiece. He has created us anew in Christ Jesus, so we can do the good things he planned for us long ago.*

God's perfection and humankind's total imperfection created a scenario that was unsolvable from our side. God, who is ultimate grace, chose to make a way. But the cross is not glorious. It was the worst possible death with unimaginable pain, rejection, and shame. How then could it change everything? Because God wrapped that terrible act in His grace. What appeared on the surface to be the very worst thing, became the greatest moment in human history – God's grace overcame sin and death and invited us into life with Him. It changes everything. There is no pearl so beautiful or priceless. There is no other way for you and me to be all we were created for, except through the grace offered in Jesus.

Jeremiah 29:11 NLT *"For I know the plans I have for you," says the LORD. "They are plans for good and not for disaster, to give you a future and a hope."*

[Hope, Pain, Perseverance, Perspective]

Chapter 21

A Snapshot of….

A SKATER?

A woman stands watching a few skaters at an indoor skating rink in a mall. She approaches the skating rink hesitantly. Nothing in her appearance would imply she belongs here. She looks homeless, wrapped in several layers of clothing and wearing heavy boots. She carries several overstuffed bags that look like they contain all her earthly possessions. Perhaps they do.

She stands at the edge of the rink watching a young woman glide across the ice—graceful, skilled, beautiful. Since childhood she has dreamed of being a skater, has felt inside that she was made for it. She stares with a sadness that has simmered for years deep in her heart, and over those years she has added on layers of clothing, her muscles have gone slack, and her heart no longer dreams. Still, she rents a pair of skates. They feel awkward and unnatural, but she approaches the rink. As she steps onto the ice, this woman is a skater. Simply because she has skates and is on the ice—she is a skater. Yet for her to truly be the skater that her heart longs to be, she will have to make some changes.

This snapshot speaks to the human condition, really. We so often live with unfulfilled hopes and dreams and thoughts of *if only, someday, I can't,* or *not my fault.* We wish for better or different, but we don't take steps to change. We allow the stuff of life to weigh us down, crush our hopes, and rob us. To be clear, I'm not talking about pipe dreams or fantasies. I can wish all day that I were a jockey: I'm five-foot-nine and weigh more than one hundred pounds (that's all you're getting), I am a woman of a certain age, and I have arthritis. Being a jockey is not a realistic dream.

But there are things I dream and desire for myself: to be healthier and more fit, to make a difference, to be active, to honor God. Simply wanting them will not make them a reality, but there are steps I can take now so that one day they might be. Unfortunately, the things I can do require discipline and commitment, like eating right, walking, perhaps exercise, taking a class, joining a team or volunteering somewhere. These are things I can do.

Consider our woman at the rink. On day one, she sets down her bags and puts on skates. Maybe she hangs onto the wall and circles once before she's exhausted and removes her skates and leaves. On day two, perhaps she takes off her heavy coat and circles the rink again, but this time she's able to glide a little without hanging on to the wall. By day three—you get the idea. Before long, she is skating—sometimes quite awkwardly—but she keeps at it and becomes healthier and stronger, more herself. She may never be an Olympian, but she goes from defeated dreamer and sad observer to spending her days doing what she was made for. You see, even before she ever started skating, she was a skater. She was made for this; she just hadn't realized it.

You and I are meant to live in the freedom of who we were created to be, and to live our best life. Whether that means becoming something new or getting rid of what weighs us down, we are made for freedom. A part of my journey has been fighting my addiction to food—it's my pacifier, my anesthetic, my comfort, and my answer to every emotional need. This has not worked well for me. Gaining freedom in this area is like setting down the bags, taking off the boots, and removing a few layers of excess clothing. Learning to deal with my emotions in a healthy way is like putting on the skates and stepping onto the ice. Awkward, for sure, a bit scary, and certainly not smooth. But it is a start toward my freedom.

What is it you want? Who do you want to be? Put down the excess baggage, put on some skates and get on the ice. Start somewhere. Do something. It's time to move past just wishing and hoping.

Ultimate freedom in this life and the next comes solely in our relationship with Jesus. A *yes* to God through Jesus is the source and power for us to live truly free. We are created to be free of addictions, shame, evil and all that robs us of our best life. The ability to live free of all that works against us is found in the power of God within us, giving us the desire and ability to live well. Oh, how I want this for you, and for me.

Further Reading

Philippians 2:13 *For God is working in you, giving you the desire and the power to do what pleases him.*

Galatians 6:9 *So let's not get tired of doing what is good. At just the right time we will reap a harvest of blessing if we don't give up.*

Psalm 139:23-24 *Search me, O God, and know my heart; test me and know my anxious thoughts. Point out anything in me that offends you, and lead me along the path of everlasting life.*

Hebrews 12:1-3 *Therefore, since we are surrounded by such a huge crowd of witnesses to the life of faith, let us strip off every weight that slows us down, especially the sin that so easily hinders our progress. And let us run with endurance the race that God has set before us. We do this by keeping our eyes on Jesus, on whom our faith depends from start to finish. He was willing to die a shameful death on the cross because of the joy he knew would be his afterward. Now he is seated in the place of highest honor beside God's throne in heaven. Think about all he endured when sinful people did such terrible things to him, so that you don't become weary and give up.*

1 John 3:1 *See how very much our Father loves us, for he calls us his children, and that is what we are!*

Romans 8:15 *So you have not received a spirit that makes you fearful slaves. Instead, you received God's Spirit when he adopted you as his own children. Now we call him, "Abba, Father."*

[Choices, Freedom, Hope, Transformation]

Chapter 22

A Snapshot of....

REDEMPTION

In the 1960s and 70s, before customer loyalty cards and online discount coupons, there were redemption stamps—Blue Chip, S&H Green Stamps, and others. When you purchased almost any product or service you could receive stamps based on the amount of your purchase. It is said that even some funeral homes and brothels gave stamps as incentive to customers.

Every time we bought groceries, gas, or about anything else, we were handed a batch of stamps. At home I licked the stamps and put them in the redemption books I was collecting. About a year into my marriage, I had finally collected enough Blue Chip Stamp books and was downright giddy as I drove to the nearest Blue Chip Stamp Redemption Center. There I searched the catalog and selected two brand new tennis rackets that arrived a week later. I traded a pile of paper, ink and spit for my new tennis rackets.

That is redemption—trading something of seemingly little value for something of greater value.

In California, when you purchase soda cans or bottles you are charged a "redemption fee." Basically, you pay up front for the use of recyclable materials like plastic, glass, and aluminum. When the cans or bottles are empty you turn them into a recycling/redemption center and you get money! The containers are no longer of any use to me but they are worth something to others. I have a friend who collects recyclables for a woman he met at a park who uses that as her sole means of income. She was homeless and now has a place to live. I keep my recyclables and give them to him, for her. What has little to no value for me has great value to her. That, too, is redemption.

Forgiveness can be a form of redemption. You trade bitterness for peace and offer others freedom from your judgment. Financial assistance, given or received, offers redemption from the weight of heavy debt. Even a meal given to a hungry person is an offer to exchange their lack for your plenty. Redemption is looking at all we have and offering something to those for whom it can be a life-changer. When we are in need of redemption, it is our willingness to accept what is offered in the name of love and mercy.

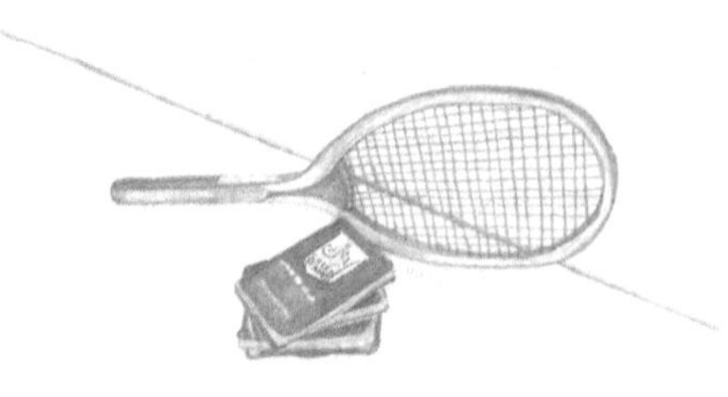

Of course, the greatest redemption story of all time and for all time is the exchange of our brokenness for God's wholeness, our limitations for His limitless love and power, our fear for His peace, our depression for His hope—I could go on. If you know anything of the Christmas story and the Easter story, you know about Jesus. Born in a stable and nailed to a cross. His story and His life are all about redemption.

Redemption is my story…

I've shared in these pages about how abuse, poverty, alcoholism, marriage issues, and so much more were a part of my younger life. But I am not the sum total of all of that brokenness. Why? Redemption. I chose to offer this mess that is me (paper, ink and spit, if you will) to the One who makes all things new. I have not one day been sorry I made the exchange. His life for me and in me is much sweeter than anything I could have planned or pulled off on my own.

Whatever your story, and whatever your faith history may be, what does redemption look like for you? Is there an area of your life that could use redeeming? Is there a way you could use your skills and resources to offer someone hope and even redemption? Whatever days you and I have on this planet, what we do for the sake of others gives more purpose in life than almost anything else. And when our days here come to a close, redemption through Jesus is what guarantees our eternity.

Further Reading

2 Corinthians 8:12 *Whatever you give is acceptable if you give it eagerly. And give according to what you have, not what you don't have.*

Romans 12:7-8 *If your gift is serving others, serve them well. If you are a teacher, teach well. If your gift is to encourage others, be encouraging. If it is giving, give generously. If God has given you leadership ability, take the responsibility seriously. And if you have a gift for showing kindness to others, do it gladly*

Isaiah 43:1-2 *"But now, O Jacob, listen to the LORD who created you. O Israel, the one who formed you says, 'Do not be afraid, for I have ransomed you, I have called you by name; you are mine. When you go through deep waters, I will be with you. When you go through rivers of difficulty, you will not drown. When you walk through the fire of oppression, you will not be burned up; the flames will not consume you.' "*

Romans 3:22-25 *We are made right with God by placing our faith in Jesus Christ. And this is true for everyone who believes, no matter who we are. For everyone has sinned; we all fall short of God's glorious standard. Yet God, in his grace, freely makes us right in his sight. He did this through Christ Jesus when he freed us from the penalty for our sins. For God presented Jesus as the sacrifice for sin. People are made right with God when they believe that Jesus sacrificed his life, shedding his blood.*

[Forgiveness, Grace, Redemption, Restoration]

Chapter 23

A Snapshot of....

A WORTHY STRUGGLE

One of the more magical events in nature is the transformation of a caterpillar into a butterfly. The delicate, colorful and graceful creature flits from flower to flower making everything seem more alive and beautiful. But how does it make that transformation?

I don't pretend to be a scientific genius, but I've always been intrigued by the process. In essence, the caterpillar spins a cocoon called a chrysalis, in which the caterpillar body breaks down completely and dies. A new body is formed from those very cells—a butterfly. The butterfly must work its way out of the chrysalis or cocoon. In the process, blood is pumped into its beautiful wings, giving it the ability to fly. If you try to help by cracking open the chrysalis yourself, the butterfly will never fly. The very act of breaking out is what gives the butterfly its ability to fly.

What a picture for us! So often we want to be bailed out of difficult situations of our own making, promising ourselves that we won't get snagged in those bad habits or consequences again. But I've found that it's the very discipline of breaking out of bad behaviors and patterns that gives us the ability to live in freedom from then on. I used to pray that God would make me skinny as I slept and promised to stay that way afterwards.

I know a young woman who was in a very difficult marriage for several years where there was infidelity, financial mismanagement, and utter lack of support. She finally had to get out of the marriage for the sake of her child as well as her own well-being. For several years she diligently worked, paid off all debt, and built a new life with great friends and family. After a few years she remarried and still lives a modest but financially sound life. God has blessed her so much with a wonderful husband, family, and home. It was a very difficult time getting out of that "cocoon" of debt but the disciplines she learned in that time have served her well.

A couple years ago I made the decision to change the way I interact with food. It had become my go-to answer for everything: boredom, celebration, sadness, sickness, always, food was my first response. In these last couple of years, I have learned to enjoy food but not worship it. Had I woken up skinny (as I had prayed) I would have had no tools to live free of food's merciless hold on me. In my marriage, the years Budd and I worked on communication, finances, parenting and conflict resolution paid off in the peaceful, sane years of his retirement before he died. We needed to break out of our own chrysalises as well as our joint one! We developed the necessary tools with much work and much prayer. All of it was worth it.

I don't know what you face these days that feels like a cocoon or place of death for you, but don't give up. I encourage you not to try and find the fastest way out, but rather the best way out. Let your difficult situation be the very training ground to learn tools and habits that lead you to life and freedom. Get whatever help you need, but also put in the work of transformation. Caterpillars may be cute, but butterflies are beautiful, free, and life-giving. It is a worthy journey for that fuzzy worm.

Further Reading

Proverbs 4:5-7 *Get wisdom; develop good judgment. Don't forget my words or turn away from them. Don't turn your back on wisdom, for she will protect you. Love her, and she will guard you. Getting wisdom is the wisest thing you can do! And whatever else you do, develop good judgment.*

Philippians 1:6 *And I am certain that God, who began the good work within you, will continue his work until it is finally finished on the day when Christ Jesus returns.*

Proverbs 3:5-6 *Trust in the Lord with all your heart; do not depend on your own understanding. Seek his will in all you do, and he will show you which path to take.*

Psalm 51:10 *Create in me a clean heart, O God. Renew a loyal spirit within me.*

Isaiah 40:31 *But those who trust in the LORD will find new strength. They will soar high on wings like eagles. They will run and not grow weary. They will walk and not faint.*

Romans 12:2 *Don't copy the behavior and customs of this world, but let God transform you into a new person by changing the way you think. Then you will learn to know God's will for you, which is good and pleasing and perfect.*

[Courage, Habits, Perseverance, Transformation]

Chapter 24

A Snapshot of....

An Unfortunate Win

My son is tall. In junior high and high school, he enjoyed basketball (still does) and I became obsessed with getting him a basketball hoop for Christmas. I desperately wanted him to be able to play any time he wanted, to be the house where his friends would gather. This was my *best idea ever*.

There was one hitch: our driveway was about fifty feet long at about a forty-degree incline. At the top, in front of the garage door, was a semi-level area about twelve feet square, three sides of which dropped off considerably. Unless you made every shot and rebound perfectly, there was a good chance you were going to be running—a lot. If the ball made it down the driveway or over the edge you had the incline of the street to deal with. If you weren't fast enough you could end up a quarter mile away dodging traffic on Foothill Boulevard.

Yes, these were issues, but why let such trivialities get in the way of your dreams? Budd and I had more than one "discussion" about my basketball dreams for Matt. He kept harping on the topography, but I was committed to the joy I foresaw and prevailed. We got the hoop, and Budd and his brother installed it. I was ecstatic. It was perfect. Ten minutes later, with Matt running up and down the driveway, fetching the ball from over the wall, arguing about who had to retrieve the rapidly departing basketball, I had my first glimpse of the question: *Was this a good idea?*

Now, you may look at this snapshot and think, *Big duh! That's not going to work.* Here's the thing: I wanted this so badly for my son that I couldn't bear to question the wisdom of my plan. I wanted the picture in my head to be our reality, so I pushed forward, despite wisdom offered to the contrary. I wanted what I wanted, period. Probably more than Matt did. As Dr. Phil would say, "How's that workin' for ya?" It didn't. Granted, we did have some fun playing there, but the seeds of my dream never grew as I pictured. Clearly, our driveway was not basketball-friendly.

I would like to say that that is the only time I pushed forward with what I wanted despite collective opinion and information to the contrary. Whether relationships, purchases, plans, or words, I have so many examples of a stubborn heart wanting what it wants when it wants it. At my current "maturity," I know that I am better with seeking wisdom and practicing patience, in part because I am older and slower. But I've also learned from the debacles in my past.

When you find yourself wanting something badly, I encourage you to pause, exhale, and consider options. Whether it's a financial matter where you want to bulldoze forward despite consequences, or a relationship that you're going to pursue or discard no matter what, take time to consider. If it's something you simply must have without question, or words you want to spew without regard to their power, I urge you to pause. Wait. Consider. Even pray.

Recently, I was hurt by someone's response to me. I had so many words—pointed, descriptive, directed, winning words. They burned in my belly and simply *had* to be expressed. But I waited (thank you God, old age, and experience). I turned the hurt over in my heart, I played with the words in my mind and I waited. Ultimately, I was able to have a conversation that did not blow up a friendship or cause me regret. I expressed myself with honesty and grace (God's doing, of course). I am so grateful for the pause.

May the wisdom of the basketball hoop guide you today. Is there something you want so badly you refuse to look at it from all sides? Is there something you want at all costs? Trust me, the cost is probably more than you anticipate. You may need to listen to wisdom from another person, even if it's your spouse. As you pause and consider, you are developing character and life skills. You are becoming the better version of yourself.

Further Reading

James 1:5 *If you need wisdom, ask our generous God, and he will give it to you. He will not rebuke you for asking.*

Proverbs 3:13-14 *Joyful is the person who finds wisdom, the one who gains understanding. For wisdom is more profitable than silver, and her wages are better than gold.*

James 3:17 *But the wisdom from above is first of all pure. It is also peace loving, gentle at all times, and willing to yield to others. It is full of mercy and the fruit of good deeds. It shows no favoritism and is always sincere.*

Proverbs 4:7 *Getting wisdom is the wisest thing you can do! And whatever else you do, develop good judgment.*

Ecclesiastes 2:13 *I thought, "Wisdom is better than foolishness, just as light is better than darkness."*

[Choices, Patience, Self-Control, Wisdom]

Chapter 25

A Snapshot of….

DANGEROUS BUMPER STICKERS

We have become something of a bumper sticker society. We speak in marketing slogans and campaign sound bites. "Just do it" was great encouragement when my toddler was standing on the side of the pool being invited to jump into my arms, but not the solution to every single challenge we face. Often slogans are fun and endearing, like, "Proud parent of a kindergarten graduate!" or "UCLA All the Way" (or USC, if you prefer). I don't do bumper stickers, but I'm often tempted to put an In-N-Out Burger sticker on my car. Some things are just really important.

I have two particular issues with bumper-sticker language. First, we too often use it as a jab or weapon against other people. We don't want a conversation; we want to speak our mind and walk away. We judge others on their response to our words, without clarification, explanation, or allowance for differences. I'm not talking literal bumper stickers now, but rather the way we talk to and about people on issues that matter to us. "Make America Great Again" might be a great campaign slogan, but what does it mean to an individual? Who decides what makes America great? When it was great was it great for everyone? "Black Lives Matter" is absolutely the truth, they do matter profoundly. But does everyone who says it mean the same thing? "Love Wins." I certainly hope so. But what exactly does it mean? Are you saying, "I'm tired of all the hate and anger; I think if we learn how to love others, we can become the kind of people we want to be," or are you saying, "Don't be bound by conventional moral boundaries, go love whoever you want, whenever you want." And what do you mean by love?

We can't possibly know everyone's story and the hurt and trauma they've suffered. If a husband abandons his wife and kids "for love," does love really win? You may respond, "That's not what I mean." Exactly. It requires a conversation. The bottom line is that these and others are complex issues and bumper sticker language can't possibly communicate all the nuance. I am not talking about acceptance of any form of abuse, violence, or hate, but about how we as individuals and a culture learn how to communicate in helpful, healing ways.

This might sound like a tirade, and perhaps it is. But in recent times we've all witnessed too much dissension and division fueled by statements made without openness or a desire for conversation. I assure you, there are issues that need changing and our collective attention. What if we stopped using our words (whether spoken or written) to throw a punch, and instead used them to extend a hand? I'm not suggesting we come to common agreement on all issues, only that we learn to listen and communicate more constructively.

A second issue I have with our bumper-sticker culture is that we have begun to make it our identity. I've known people who could get in a physical fight over their college allegiance. Seriously, people, it's a school! In 2011 a man was beaten almost to death by some Dodger fans because he was a Giants fan. Unbelievable. When our identity is derived from such things, we must seriously question who we are and what we represent. If being a Republican or a Democrat is the most important thing about you then I pray you find more for your life. If the way you look is the most important thing about you then I pray you discover what it means to be formed in God's image, and realize that those who don't look like you are also formed in His image. God has a very big image. Perhaps you need to expand your list of people who God loves to include everyone. If you are too easily offended by or defensive of someone's "bumper sticker," your identity may be somewhat misplaced. You may need to ask yourself: What is the most important thing about me?

We can be people who speak with conviction as well as grace and patience. Take time to try and understand even the people that may offend you or threaten the truth as you see it. Resist the urge to slap a bumper sticker and an identity on anyone else. It doesn't take a lot, just the willingness to allow for differences. Tempering our language, our emotions, and our thoughts can lead to peace in us and through us. Consider today where your primary identity lies. Do you even know? Are you willing to reach out, even just a little bit, to someone who thinks differently than you do?

I pray you will first find the deep, deep love of God for you, and in that love find the capacity to love others. God's love can heal, restore, and shape your life. He truly is the Truth that changes everything.

Further Reading

John 4:1-42 is the telling of Jesus' encounter with a Samaritan woman. Jews and Samaritans were at odds and did not like each other. Jews considered Samaritans 'dogs.' And yet Jesus engages this woman in conversation that leads her to faith, acceptance, and even bringing many in her town to know and accept Jesus. It was a conversation rather than dueling bumper stickers.

Luke 19:1-10 tells of Zaccheus, a tax collector, which made him utterly hated by the Jews. Jesus invites himself to the man's house, much to the anger of the religious leaders. Jesus initiated a conversation that led to radical change and redemption.

Acts 15:8-11 records an issue raised in the first Christian church regarding what it takes to be accepted by God. Some early church leaders wanted to make Gentiles follow Jewish laws in order to be accepted. It took a prayerful and diligent conversation to arrive at a gracious plan.

Galatians 3:28 *There is no longer Jew or Gentile, slave or free, male and female. For you are all one in Christ Jesus.*

[Acceptance, Communication, Identity, Relationships]

Chapter 26

A Snapshot of....

A TIRESOME MERRY-GO-ROUND

Families: Fabulous. Messy. Beautiful. Painful.

I have three sisters. We are close and enjoy being together when we can, though we are spread from coast to coast. When together, we tell stories that grow with the retelling and we laugh a lot. Mom was always surprised by the stories that, apparently, she wasn't aware of at the time. Every now and then, a situation will spark something between us, and I find myself reverting to my childhood role, issues, and responses. I almost expect to hear myself say, "I'm telling Mom!" It's a very strange phenomenon.

I have seen this same pattern present in other families. A friend who's grown with a family of her own recently told me she's going "home" for the holidays, and was hesitant to face the uncomfortable family dynamics that have not changed since her childhood. I told her about a picture I have in my mind of a merry-go-round. When people get together it only takes one person to bring up an old grievance, to accuse someone, or to harp on touchy issues. These old patterns are like the music that accompanies a merry-go-round. As soon as that music begins, the family climbs onto the merry-go-round and we go round-and-round-and-round, airing old grievances, arguing or blaming, or getting offended. The yellers yell. The cold and withdrawn families fracture and drift apart. The drinkers bring out the alcohol to numb the tensions. Family dynamics are like a long-running merry-go-round. I suggested to my friend, "When you hear the music, don't get on the merry-go-round." In essence, choose not to engage in old patterns that are hurtful and unhelpful.

A couple of weeks later, I got a call from my friend. "I hear the music! I hear the music!" It took a second for me to put context to her proclamation. *Oh!* "I didn't get on the merry-go-round! I didn't get on!" It was so fun to hear her talk about how she didn't engage in old patterns and consequently wasn't upset or wounded. She chose her role and held to it. It was a huge victory for her.

Family dynamics are influenced and shaped by so many things: generational habits (good and bad), addictions, sound faith (or lack of it), bitterness that has never been dealt with, losses through death, divorce, or abandonment, and on it goes. We cannot control or erase all of the negative influences that have shaped our family, but we can choose what we will carry forward. What healthy patterns and traditions can you practice, in your own home, and at your next gathering?

Centrifugal force is power that draws you away from the center when something begins to spin, like a playground merry-go-round you push to make it go faster and faster. When a merry-go-round speeds up, like the negative family dynamics my friend was dreading, things begin to slide off. In this case, things like grace, forgiveness, kindness, sanity are usually the first to go. As tensions and words react to the familiar pressures, the healthy responses we've been developing get sucked out of us until we're just hanging on to this destructive merry-go-round. Don't lose who you are becoming. When you hear the music, don't get on.

My daughter-in-law once said to me, "Thanks for teaching your son to talk through *everything*." Her playful smirk told me it wasn't always an easy trait for someone who didn't grow up with a mother like me. Thankfully, she loves me and lets me talk through *everything*. Airing our thoughts and feelings, as much as we know how to, is a part of our family dynamic—good or bad, it's what happens on our merry-go-round.

As I've said before, my grandfather was an alcoholic and an abuser. A huge part of that family dynamic was silence and secrets. Perhaps that's why I have a need to keep things in the open. I never want to lose my voice or hide in the shadows again. I admit, I may overdo it sometimes. I seem to have a lot of words.

Whether in your family of origin, workplace team, or circle of friends, there is probably a familiar pattern of interaction. It might be extreme competitiveness at your job, or jealousy rearing its ugly head among your friends. You don't have to engage. Don't let others determine who you will be or how you will react. Learn and practice patience, forgiveness, kindness, gentleness, all those wonderful qualities that keep our heart and mind at peace. There may be countless unhealthy and unhappy merry-go-rounds in your life, but you don't have to get on them. Stand your ground. God will help, He always does.

Further Reading

Matthew 22:38-40 MSG *Jesus said, "'Love the Lord your God with all your passion and prayer and intelligence.' This is the most important, the first on any list. But there is a second to set alongside it: 'Love others as well as you love yourself.' These two commands are pegs; everything in God's Law and the Prophets hangs from them."*

Colossians 3:13 *Make allowance for each other's faults, and forgive anyone who offends you. Remember, the Lord forgave you, so you must forgive others.*

Romans 12:9 *Don't just pretend to love others. Really love them. Hate what is wrong. Hold tightly to what is good.*

Romans 12:18 *Do all that you can to live in peace with everyone.*

Galatians 5:22-23 *But the Holy Spirit produces this kind of fruit in our lives: love, joy, peace, patience, kindness, goodness, faithfulness, gentleness, and self-control…*

[Choices, Family, Peace, Rest]

Chapter 27

A Snapshot of....

A PURPOSEFUL ENDURANCE

You probably understand life fully. Maybe you are one of those people who nods and smiles no matter what comes your way. I'm happy for you. Sadly, that's not me. I mull and wonder and go over everything in my head believing that I can make sense of it, then be able to fix it easily. You're probably thinking that is fantasy. My experience would prove you right.

In a particularly tough season of life centered mostly on the challenges in my marriage, I was pondering, thinking, and praying one evening. If I could just figure out exactly what was broken between Budd and me, I could fix it and we would be golden, finally. But the solution refused to appear. I was so very tired and hopeless. As I fretted, I saw a picture in my mind's eye that was strange even for me!

In my picture, I was standing on an asphalt path, like a cart path at a golf course, that stretched out before me like a black ribbon into beautiful green rolling hills. Standing on the side of this path was a *very* strange creature with a demon-like face that looked something like a hyena. The creature was wearing a big fruit turban, like actress Carmen Miranda used to wear in movies, and a dress made up entirely of garish colorful ruffles. It wore pantaloons made of the same bright ruffles and was doing a can-can dance with the yips and howls that apparently accompany can-can dances. (You, too, are probably thinking that I should have gotten help immediately.)

As I stood there on the path, staring in amazement at this creature, I felt God speak to my heart something like this: "Kathy, the enemy of your soul cannot come on the path that I have created for you, nor can he pull you from this path that leads to your best life. But he can distract you enough that you don't grow or move forward into all that I have for you. You don't have to be stuck here."

Wow. It was a powerful moment, and I suddenly realized how stuck I had become. I was so busy trying to fix the stuff of my everyday life that I failed to really lean into God, trust Him to know what's best, and to provide it. I was defining my life by its problems and unable to move ahead, as though, as soon as I fixed my marriage, everything else would be good to go. Life doesn't work that way. I chose at that moment to turn and walk away from the distraction and renew my pursuit of God's love and life for me.

Please understand, I am not saying we should ignore issues and just blow them off. Not at all. But I do believe we can become so fixated on what is not good that we miss out on all the possibilities available to us. When I stopped fixating on the difficulties in my marriage and began to pursue personal wholeness in the form of therapy, health awareness, enjoying my kids, owning my "junk," etc., I found my relationship with Budd began to change. Apparently, shockingly, I was a part of the problem, and my stuck-ness was not helping. Go figure.

I didn't intend to get so focused on the problems, but found myself there nonetheless. Whether it is a relationship, job, finances, health, or any of the myriad of life events that keep us from joy and peace, we choose how much power we give them to define our life. Endurance isn't just "hanging on 'til Jesus comes," it is a mindset that presses forward, learning and growing through the stuff and stages of life. Don't let the worst part of your life define your present or your future, even if it defined your past. With God's help, stop staring at the ugly thing doing the can-can dance and move on to life as it's meant to be lived.

Further Reading

Philippians 1:9-11 *I pray that your love will overflow more and more, and that you will keep on growing in knowledge and understanding. For I want you to understand what really matters, so that you may live pure and blameless lives until the* *day of Christ's return. May you always be filled with the fruit of your salvation—the righteous character produced in your life by Jesus Christ—for this will bring much glory and praise to God.*

Hosea 14:9 *Let those who are wise understand these things. Let those with discernment listen carefully. The paths of the Lord are true and right, and righteous people live by walking in them. But in those paths sinners stumble and fall.*

James 3:13-18 MSG *Do you want to be counted wise, to build a reputation for wisdom? Here's what you do: Live well, live wisely, live humbly. It's the way you live, not the way you talk, that counts. Mean-spirited ambition isn't wisdom. Boasting that you are wise isn't wisdom. Twisting the truth to make yourselves sound wise isn't wisdom. It's the furthest thing from wisdom—it's animal cunning, devilish plotting. Whenever you're trying to look better than others or get the better of others, things fall apart and everyone ends up at the others' throats.*

Real wisdom, God's wisdom, begins with a holy life and is characterized by getting along with others. It is gentle and reasonable, overflowing with mercy and blessings, not hot one day and cold the next, not two-faced. You can develop a healthy, robust community that lives right with God and enjoy its results only if you do the hard work of getting along with each other, treating each other with dignity and honor.

[Choices, Courage, Marriage, Perseverance]

Chapter 28

A Snapshot of....

A Cautious Page Turning

When I was young, I loved looking through *National Geographic* magazines at the mesmerizing pictures of mountains, oceans, forests, desserts, flowers, all aspects of nature. Some of the pictures, however, were scary. I'd turn a page and a full-spread close-up of some weird fish with fangs and bug eyes would pop out at me. It scared me to death and gave me the creeps. So, I learned to turn each page very slowly from the bottom corner and peek at it carefully until I was sure it was safe. If it looked threatening, I didn't turn it. Sometimes I'd hold the book as far away as possible, peek through one eye and slowly turn the page, always trying to prepare for the scary stuff.

Life can be a lot like *National Geographic* magazine: it can be scary to turn pages, to adjust to big changes, or to imagine life after losing someone or something important like a spouse, child, parent, job, or home. What a huge and frightening page to turn! And yet, we must, because life doesn't stop for us, even when it feels as though it should. In the fifteen years since Budd passed away there have been many pages I haven't wanted to turn, but life keeps moving forward. I'm grateful for God's kindness and the good life I have. I've kept turning the page and it hasn't ruined me, it has grown me.

I recently sold the house where we raised our family. It is a great house but was too much for me. That was a big page to turn. It required accepting unfamiliar things that, with time, are now becoming familiar. God knew what He was asking and, not surprisingly, He has been right about every single page. The Bible is filled with stunning stories of disappointment, loss, and risky page turning:

— Adam and Eve, because of their own failures, had to leave their perfect home for a wasteland. (Genesis 2-3)

— Noah was serving God and raising a family when God suddenly called him to become a zoo-keeping sailor. Oh, and save humanity. (Genesis 6-8)

— Joseph was the favored son who ended up thrown in a hole then sold into slavery by his bros. (Genesis 37 and 39-50 if you want the whole story!)

— David, a young shepherd, was anointed to be King of Israel then sent back to tend his sheep for years. (1 Samuel 16)

- — Mary, a young Jewish girl, is told she's a pregnant virgin but not to worry, it's God's child. I wonder what her first thoughts were the morning after she found out? (Luke 1:26-38)
- — Paul was passionate about the God of Israel until Jesus knocked him off his donkey and changed the course of his life. (Acts 9:1-31)

How did any of these people manage to turn the page before them? How does one accept and acclimate to such mystery, loss, and drastic change? The common denominator is God. They all chose to trust that God knew what He was doing. God is neither surprised nor put off by the pages that lie ahead of us, any more than He is limited by the pages we've already turned. God, in Jesus, left His throne and came to walk the dusty paths of the Middle East, only to be misunderstood, rejected, tortured and murdered. How does one turn that page? God is always good and invites us to trust Him with the next stages and pages of our life.

Turning pages is most difficult when the future looks bleak or uncertain. Life done in our own wisdom and strength can be brutal, but if we believe that God is good and already knows our tomorrows, we can confidently turn the next page, even if we only do it a peek at a time. I've never been sorry I trusted Him. Ever.

Further Reading

Jeremiah 29:11 "*For I know the plans I have for you," says the* L*ORD*. "*They are plans for good and not for disaster, to give you a future and a hope.*"

Psalm 40: 5 *O Lord my God, you have performed many wonders for us. Your plans for us are too numerous to list. You have no equal. If I tried to recite all your wonderful deeds, I would never come to the end of them.*

Isaiah 41:10,13 *Don't be afraid, for I am with you. Don't be discouraged, for I am your God. I will strengthen you and help you. I will hold you up with my victorious right hand. For I hold you by your right hand — I, the Lord your God. And I say to you, 'Don't be afraid. I am here to help you.'*

Isaiah 55:8-9 *"My thoughts are nothing like your thoughts," says the Lord. "And my ways are far beyond anything you could imagine. For just as the heavens are higher than the earth, so my ways are higher than your ways and my thoughts higher than your thoughts."*

[Courage, Perseverance, Transformation, Trust]

Chapter 29

A Snapshot of....

A Major Reboot

I have a love/hate relationship with computers. When they work and make sense, they are amazingly fun and useful. These days, online connection like Zoom bring teams, families, and friends together as never before. When technology doesn't cooperate, which can happen by a single keystroke, it becomes the source of all evil in my life. That may be an exaggeration.

Decades ago, I was asked to write Kids' Church curriculum on the church's new computer, the first computer I'd ever seen up-close or touched. It was not a bad idea, in theory. After hours of learning to turn it on and find the word processor (this was pre-Microsoft or Apple), I began to write. I poured my heart and brain into an idea and began to develop it. And *then*. I hit a wrong key and either lost it to eternity or it began to "loop" itself, repeating over and over. This happened several times. One particularly rough session I ended up sobbing, literally. I was sure God didn't love me, my church was trying to drive me insane, and my children loved a different mother. Yes, I can get dramatic at times.

I called over the co-worker who had suggested this computer thing. He touched a couple of buttons and everything was as it should be. I punched him in the stomach. Okay, I didn't punch him, but I didn't hug him either. I had done everything I knew to do, and it only made things worse.

Several years later in a very difficult season of my life, things began to unravel for me. My marriage was on sharp rocks, my kids were okay, but I wasn't connecting well with them, I was weighed down trying to be a good church girl, and none of my friends were aware of it. I felt like a terrible wife, an inept mother, a pathetic Christ-follower, and a lousy friend. I prayed, cried, and begged God to fix things. Full disclosure: I asked God to take me to heaven in my sleep and give Budd and my kids a better wife/mother. I was done.

This "season" carried on for far too long. Then one evening after a church service I felt like God spoke to me through a picture in my mind. I saw an old computer mainframe, the big kind like in old movies, and it was unplugged. I felt God saying to me, "Kathy, I have to unplug the computer that is you so I can reprogram it." God may have been whispering to me prior to this encounter, but

I was so busy being "good" I couldn't pause long enough to listen. So God took bold action: He unplugged me.

My limited wife skills were depleted. My mothering was more survival than thriving, my Christian life was dependent on my performance, and my friends were kept in the dark. With no other power source, I surrendered to the outage. This began a season of deconstruction of my beliefs about God and myself. Over time I gave up on trying to be good and focused on learning who God truly is and loving Him with my whole heart. I asked God to show me how to love my husband. I began the process of loving my children as God's little people and not as extensions of myself. One of the biggest things I learned was how to love myself—my weird, self-centered, broken self.

As the fruit of this new way of thinking began to take root, I realized that for the outside observer my life probably didn't look that different, but inside everything had changed. I was learning to act out of the abundance of God's grace in me, not trying to deserve it. You see, God loves you and me exactly as we are. That's grace! The changes I encountered did not make God love me more, but rather made it possible for me to experience His gracious love for me. It changed the why and how of the way I live my life. I no longer need everyone's approval in order to feel that I matter, at least not as much. I'm still a work in progress.

Do you feel unplugged? Does it feel that everything you're doing is draining and not life-giving? As my friend who ran our Recovery Ministry once said to me, "Kathy, stop 'should-ing' all over yourself!"

I encourage you to surrender to the amazing love and grace of God. He can handle your stuff. And if you are in a difficult season, I encourage you to seek help from a pastor, counselor, or therapist; join a Bible study, support group or get people to pray for you. You don't have to navigate it alone. We're better together.

Further Reading

Romans 8:39 *No power in the sky above or in the earth below—indeed, nothing in all creation will ever be able to separate us from the love of God that is revealed in Christ Jesus our Lord.*

Psalm 29:11 *The LORD gives his people strength. The LORD blesses them with peace.*

Deuteronomy 8:16-18 *He fed you with manna in the wilderness, a food unknown to your ancestors. He did this to humble you and test you for your own good. He did all this so you would never say to yourself, 'I have achieved this wealth with my own strength and energy.' Remember the LORD your God. He is the one who gives you power to be successful, in order to fulfill the covenant he confirmed to your ancestors with an oath.*

Psalm 28:7 *The LORD is my strength and shield. I trust him with all my heart. He helps me, and my heart is filled with joy. I burst out in songs of thanksgiving.*

Psalm 29:11 *The LORD gives his people strength. The LORD blesses them with peace.*

Ephesians 3:16-17 *I pray that from his glorious, unlimited resources he will empower you with inner strength through his Spirit. Then Christ will make his home in your hearts as you trust in him. Your roots will grow down into God's love and keep you strong.*

[Brokenness, Grace, Restoration]

Chapter 30

A Snapshot of….

A Seething Volcano

Mount Vesuvius, Mount St. Helens, Mauna Loa, Krakatoa, Eyjafjallajökull. What do they have in common? They are all fairly well-known volcanoes. By definition, a volcano is an opening in the earth's crust that allows molten rock, gases, and debris to escape to the surface. A volcano is basically a mountain with a seething attitude that can or will erupt at any given moment. The fact that it looks benign or calm has nothing to do with what is churning around in its deep belly.

There are currently about fifteen hundred active volcanoes on our planet and one-hundred-sixty-nine potentially active in the US. Davis Johnston was a thirty-year-old volcanologist who was encamped and studying Mount St. Helens in Washington in 1980. Moments before his position was hit by a massive deadly blast and flow, Johnston radioed his famous last words: "Vancouver! Vancouver! This is it!" His body was never found. The pressure had been building for years and finally erupted. Davis Johnston was in its direct path.

Wouldn't it be awful if people were like volcanoes? Oh, wait, sometimes we are. During childhood we learn to do and say the appropriate things to avoid conflict, be accepted and praised, and even loved. We learn to squelch negative thoughts and feelings in favor of playing nice. As adults we learn to show our best face at work, church, with friends, and sometimes even with family. We are a lovely part of the landscape of creation, until we blow.

Several years ago Budd and I were driving home from a marriage conference. We started arguing and it escalated quickly. The tension just kept building until I screamed (I'm not usually a screamer), "I HATE YOU!" The air seemed to have been sucked out of the car and it got very quiet. Where did that come from?! It had been building for years and was tied to my childhood feeling of not being heard or protected. It took Budd and I a good deal of counseling to sort it out and get through it.

I know this topic is beyond the scope of a snapshot post, but many of us have been wounded by abuse, neglect, rejection and abandonment, and these deep wounds are often not dealt with. This means that they still hold the power to explode (or implode) our world. My desire in writing this snapshot is that you would be willing to take a bit of an inventory of your heart and mind. Are there landmines that have never been defused? For the sake of your own health and happiness, as well as the love of others, take care of the molten anger or unforgiveness that can destroy you. You may be able to suppress and swallow it for a while, but like a volcano it could one day erupt and destroy everyone in its shadow, including you.

God is always available and desires your wholeness. Therapists, counselors, pastors, and even friends can offer a gracious ear as well as a path to freedom. Volcanoes are very destructive and unpredictable. Diligently pursue peace today. Pursue a foundation that won't give way or erupt on those you love. Now is a really good time to begin that journey. Just do it.

Further Reading

Isaiah 28:12 *God has told his people, "Here is a place of rest; let the weary rest here. This is a place of quiet rest." But they would not listen.*

Matthew 11:28-29 *Then Jesus said, "Come to me, all of you who are weary and carry heavy burdens, and I will give you rest. Take my yoke upon you. Let me teach you, because I am humble and gentle at heart, and you will find rest for your souls."*

Isaiah 26:3 *You will keep in perfect peace all who trust in you, all whose thoughts are fixed on you!*

Galatians 5:22-23 *But the Holy Spirit produces this kind of fruit in our lives: love, joy, peace, patience, kindness, goodness,* *faithfulness, gentleness, and self-control. There is no law against these things!*

Psalm 29:11 *The LORD gives his people strength. The LORD blesses them with peace.*

Philippians 4:7 *Then you will experience God's peace, which exceeds anything we can understand. His peace will guard your hearts and minds as you live in Christ Jesus.*

[Anger, Freedom, Peace]

Chapter 31

Snapshot of…

An Honest Identity

What do you see in this picture?

According to Wikipedia, "The Rorschach test is a psychological test in which subjects' perceptions of inkblots are recorded and then analyzed using psychological interpretation, complex algorithms, or both. Some psychologists use this test to examine a person's personality characteristics and emotional functioning."

Okay, so this isn't really a Rorschach test and I'm not going to analyze your personality or thought processes, but I do want you to ponder this snapshot. What is it conveying to you? What's the story being told?

I used this snapshot in a teaching several years ago. It was originally intended to open a discussion on community and relationships. I was amazed to discover the vast number of ways people interpreted the picture, including these:

— The lady with the Bible is a church lady welcoming the broken woman.

— The Bible lady is acting superior and trying to get the broken woman to come to her holy way of thinking. Many people had an adverse reaction to the "holier-than-thou" woman.

— The broken woman is coming to the Bible lady for help and compassion.

— Friendships are made up of very different kinds of people.

As in most art, there isn't really a right or wrong interpretation. It's in the eye of the beholder. But since this is my snapshot, I'll tell you what I think it conveys.

You may have noticed that the women are wearing the same bracelet. To me this picture represents one person. I am both of these women. I am, at any given time, a fairly put-together person. I love God and believe in His Word. I like people and I care about their well-being. As much as it is in my power and wisdom, I like to improve others' lives. Sometimes, though, I may think I'm a bit better than another person, even though I am also a mess. There are also areas in my life that feel broken or worn down. Whether it's something basic like my love/hate relationship with food or more complicated like the judgments I hold in my heart and mind against others, I am a mess.

So, what's the point? For me, it's recognizing and owning who I really am. I am not pond-scum, nor am I an angelic being sent to grace the world with my perfection. I am not the standard by which all others should be measured. If I cling too tightly to either identification, then I fail to truly know myself and certainly fail to ever be at peace. While my weaknesses and failures frustrate and often sadden me, they do not sink my boat. I don't expect perfection of myself, and I've learned to ask for forgiveness, give forgiveness and accept myself and others as mere human beings—both delightful and difficult.

If you know God's story, you know that you are utterly loved by Him. You should also know that He is at work in every area of your life, shaping and growing you into a person who is more like Christ every day. This is my great hope, and it's what gives me the ability to accept the broken places and to be humbly grateful for who I am becoming.

If you spend a lot of emotional energy berating yourself, please stop. If you are coming to believe that you are the standard of goodness by which all others should be measured, please stop. You are a work in progress. Your friends, family, boss, and others are all works in progress. We and they are daily in desperate need of grace. Give yourself a break. Give them a break.

Further Reading

Colossians 3:10 *Put on your new nature, and be renewed as you learn to know your Creator and become like him.*

Philippians 1:3,6 *Every time I think of you, I give thanks to my God. … And I am certain that God, who began the good work within you, will continue his work until it is finally finished on the day when Christ Jesus returns.*

Psalm 51:10 *Create in me a clean heart, O God. Renew a loyal spirit within me.*

Isaiah 40:31 *But those who trust in the LORD will find new strength. They will soar high on wings like eagles. They will run and not grow weary. They will walk and not faint.*

Romans 12:2 *Don't copy the behavior and customs of this world, but let God transform you into a new person by changing the way you think. Then you will learn to know God's will for you, which is good and pleasing and perfect.*

[Acceptance, Grace, Identity, Relationships]

Chapter 32

A Snapshot of....

CLUTCHING A PANT LEG

I was chatting with a group of friends while our kids played around our feet. Suddenly I felt that wonderful feeling of little hands clutching my jeans and a head leaning against my leg. I looked down expecting to see my daughter, but it was another little girl leaning on me. I was about to stoop down to talk to her eye to eye when she looked up, at first surprised, then terrified. I was not who she expected to see! She screamed as I turned toward her mom who was already bending down to get her. For the rest of the time we stood and talked, this beautiful little cherub stared at me with utter disapproval. Somehow the whole thing was my fault and she wanted me to know it.

Over the years this snapshot has come to my mind when I find myself holding onto something or someone I expected would bring me joy, peace, or safety, only to find that it was the wrong thing or the wrong person. Perhaps it is the human condition that we reach for whatever is closest or easiest in order to fill up our sadness, fear, passions, or emptiness. I have been disappointed so many times because I ran to the wrong thing to try to make myself feel loved, important, worthy, or needed.

What makes this even worse is the fact that our culture is forever offering us an answer to all our woes. A better car, a bigger home, more money, more stuff, a facelift, or a different spouse. We look at ourselves in the mirror and see all that we deem wrong. We measure our inner thoughts and feelings against what we see in others' lives. You act kind and I feel bad that I'm not kind enough. Your marriage looks happy and I'm struggling in mine. We compare ourselves to posters, pictures, and celebrities and usually come up short. We assuage those feelings of insignificance or insecurity with things like food, alcohol, inappropriate relationships, spending, judgment, gossip—the list is truly endless.

When it all falls apart, we seem as shocked as that toddler clutching my pant leg. It's not what we expected. It isn't who we expected. And we are faced with a decision: What do I do now? If it's a relationship, we tend to move on to another one, thinking that will be the one. If it's alcohol or drugs, we use more to dull the pain and disappointment. If it's food, we gorge. If we suffer from self-loathing, we tear others down to feel better about ourselves.

It's a vicious cycle difficult to get out of. We cling to pacifiers long after we should have outgrown them.

My little "leg-grabber" was instantly rescued by her mom, safe and secure, if a bit emotionally tenuous. She was close to what she wanted and needed, but she'd missed it by a leg. God, throughout history, has spoken and proved that He is our life, our safety, our hiding place, and our provider. It is His delight to care for us and provide all good things; but too often we want to determine what those good things should be. We want what we want when we want it. And just like our children, we don't always know what's best for us. The God who made us knows exactly what He created us to be and do.

I've held a lot of pant legs in my life. I have hurt myself and others through my bad choices. But I promise you that I have never regretted the outcome of any challenge or relationship that came directly from God's direction and invitation. It may sound funny to you, but He really does know what He's doing. And He really does know you. Of all the pant legs you may reach for, He is the right one, the best pant leg you'll ever grab hold of.

Further Reading

Matthew 6:33 MSG *If God gives such attention to the appearance of wildflowers—most of which are never even seen—don't you think he'll attend to you, take pride in you, do his best for you? What I'm trying to do here is to get you to relax, to not be so preoccupied with getting, so you can respond to God's giving. People who don't know God and the way he works fuss over* *these things, but you know both God and how he works. Steep your life in God-reality, God-initiative, God-provisions. Don't worry about missing out. You'll find all your everyday human concerns will be met.*

Psalm 34:18 *The Lord is close to the brokenhearted; he rescues those whose spirits are crushed.*

Psalm 147:3 *He heals the brokenhearted and bandages their wounds.*

Isaiah 61:1-3 *The Spirit of the Sovereign Lord is upon me, for the Lord has anointed me to bring good news to the poor.*

[Choices, Faith, Trust]

Chapter 33

A Snapshot of….

LASTING FINGERPRINTS

Fingerprints. Unique in all the world. One of a kind. So unique they're used to identify both victims and criminals. Your fingerprints are yours alone, and every fingerprint you've ever left marks a place where you were, what you touched, and perhaps what you did. In a metaphorical way, we leave our fingerprints on people and they leave theirs on us. Parents, siblings, friends, spouses, kids—everyone we encounter is touched by our words and actions. We leave a mark on others. And they leave a mark on us.

Sometimes fingerprints are like scars, as in rejection, abuse, violence, bullying and such. Sometimes they are firmly shaping us like the hands of a potter on clay. Sometimes fingerprints are a delicate touch like a butterfly alighting on a flower. Whatever the case, we get to choose how we will leave our prints on the world around us. When you are at a restaurant, what fingerprint do you leave on the person who serves you? What about strangers you pass on the street? Do you ever consider leaving the fingerprint of a smile or friendly nod? It doesn't take a lot to leave a touch of warmth on another human being, especially those closest to you.

Think about your fingerprints. One of a kind, unique to you. No one else can duplicate your love, support, faithfulness, or trust. Only you have had the experiences in your life, and you bear your unique character and influence. What fingerprints do you want to leave? Today you get to start fresh. Choose it.

And what about the fingerprints left on us? What can we do about the hurtful, shaming, or scarring fingerprints that have been left on our heart and mind? How do I erase the fingerprints of my abusive grandfather or abandoning father? What do we do with the fingerprints of friends or teachers who embarrassed, hurt, or shamed us? Those are like unwanted tattoos. While they may be permanent in the sense that they did happen, they need not define who we are today.

You and I were created by a good and loving God who wants goodness for us. In fact, He promises it. It doesn't mean we don't face hard things—that's just a part of being human. But He does promise that even the painful and difficult stuff of life, when placed in His hands, can ultimately be worked for our good. We don't have to like that difficult things happen, just remember that they need not define and cripple us. This has been my experience with every challenging season of my life. God is good and can redeem brokenness.

I encourage you, and me, to acknowledge and release the painful fingerprints left on our hearts and minds. Whether through abuse or disappointments, we can let go of the things that want to mark us. I am so grateful there is a way to be free of painful marks that want to define me. It's simple but it isn't easy: acknowledge they exist, forgive the perpetrator, and release them to God. It's time to clean unwanted fingerprints. It's worth it. Acknowledge. Forgive. Release.

You might want to join me in this prayer: Lord, let the fingerprints I leave on others be tinged with grace and a thing of beauty and not pain. That requires a whole lot of You in me.

Further Reading

Ecclesiastes 10:12 *Wise words bring approval, but fools are destroyed by their own words.*

Ephesians 4:29 *...Let everything you say be good and helpful, so that your words will be an encouragement to those who hear them.*

Ephesians 4:32 *Instead, be kind to each other, tenderhearted, forgiving one another, just as God through Christ has forgiven you.*

Colossians 3:12 *Since God chose you to be the holy people he loves, you must clothe yourselves with tenderhearted mercy, kindness, humility, gentleness, and patience.*

Matthew 5:14-16 *You are the light of the world—like a city on a hilltop that cannot be hidden. No one lights a lamp and then puts it under a basket. Instead, a lamp is placed on a stand, where it gives light to everyone in the house. In the same way, let your good deeds shine out for all to see, so that everyone will praise your heavenly Father.*

Isaiah 50:4 *The Sovereign* LORD *has given me his words of wisdom, so that I know how to comfort the weary. Morning by morning he wakens me and opens my understanding to his will.*

[Forgiveness, Identity, Influence, Transformation]

Chapter 34

A Snapshot of....

A FIELD OF WEEDS

When Budd and I were in a rough season of marriage, we were disconnected, unhappy, blame-ridden, and unforgiving. It was a mess. We tried a bit of counseling but were unable to break free from our very destructive patterns. Through a recommendation from a well-respected friend, we enrolled in a program at a church. It was...challenging. On our way to the third session of what can only be called a hardcore program, Budd and I again found ourselves in an intense argument (about what, I have no idea). As we sat in this large church with hundreds of other couples, listening to more "stuff," I gave up. "God, none of this is working. We're reading the books, praying together, talking with our mentors and nothing is changing. Nothing. I'm done."

God responded with a picture of a field covered with brambles, scrub, and weeds. The gist of what I sensed God saying was this: "Kathy, you have spent years sowing seeds of pain, brokenness, and

bitterness into your life. What you see is the result of years of bad seeds coming to fullness and reproducing. But in recent months, you and Budd have begun to sow seeds that bring life. You may not see the fruit of those seeds yet, but they are taking root in the soil of your heart. Be patient and don't give up."

Budd and I spent our first ten to fifteen years together in total ignorance of the seeds we were planting in our marriage. We didn't speak honestly about everything, we sometimes pretended, we talked *about* when we should have talked *to* each other, and we kept an inner tally of the offenses we felt from the other. None of this was intentional. We simply used the tools we knew in order to cope and survive. Clearly, these were not the right tools. So, year after year, we struggled to keep our individual heads above water and in the process continued to drown the other person in judgment, lack of trust, and isolation. This was the field we were living in that day when God showed up for me.

You may be wondering if I got this beautiful "aha" moment, shared it with Budd, and we walked hand in hand down the garden path into our own personal sunset. Sorry. That's a great made-for-TV movie or romance novel but it's not real life, at least not ours. We still struggled, argued, doubted one another, and wanted to give up. But the picture of the field gave us hope. We had to trust what we couldn't see and believe what we couldn't fathom—that there was good being formed in us and between us.

It was a slow journey that required much time in counseling, prayer, apologies, and forgiveness. Interesting, though, it didn't take as long for the flowers and fruit to sprout and bloom as it had for the field to be inundated with weeds. Yes, it took time but there were enough small wins along the way to encourage us to keep going. The weeds didn't win.

I'm sure we've all heard the simplest definition of insanity as "doing the same things and expecting different results." I decide to lose weight but don't change what I eat or add exercise to my days and yet, because I decided to lose weight, I expect it to happen. Insanity. I have a gluten sensitivity that causes my sinuses to go haywire but I love bread and pasta, so I cheat all the time. Am I surprised that my sinuses are a mess? Insanity.

Budd and I were married thirty-nine years and raised two amazing kids who have given us four fabulous grandchildren. Beautiful fruit from what had once been a field of weeds. God's abundance does not limit what we can be or do. I have been deeply changed because I didn't bail on my marriage, nor did Budd. I have learned and am learning daily that God's timing is perfect (though, I'll admit, always too slow for me), and that He is powerful in His ability and desire to heal and restore.

Don't give up. Whatever the field that is your life looks like today, it does not have to define your tomorrows. Don't get tired of doing the right thing, whether that is a relationship, a healthier lifestyle, developing character, better habits, or a more God-focused life. As you press on, one day you will see the beautiful fruit of your commitment. Don't quit on your best life. Don't quit on God.

Further Reading

Galatians 6:7,9-10 *Make no mistake: God can't be mocked. What you give is what you get. What you sow, you harvest.... May we never tire of doing what is good and right before our Lord because in His season we shall bring in a great harvest if we can just persist. So seize any opportunity the Lord gives you to do good things and be a blessing to everyone, especially those within our faithful family.*

Hebrews 12:1-3 *Since we have such a huge crowd of people of faith watching us from the grandstands, let us strip off anything that slows us down or holds us back, and especially those sins that wrap themselves so tightly around our feet and trip us up; and let us run with patience the particular race that God has set before us. Keep your eyes on Jesus, our leader and instructor. He was willing to die a shameful death on the cross because of the joy he knew would be his afterwards; and now he sits in the place of honor by the throne of God. If you want to keep from* *becoming fainthearted and weary, think about his patience as sinful men did such terrible things to him.*

[Choices, Marriage, Perseverance, Trust]

Chapter 35

A Snapshot of....

A HARD AND FAITHFUL LIFE

When my sister Barbara was about nine months old, she had a bad case of impetigo (red, scabby sores all over her body). My mom, a twenty-two-year-old single mother of three girls, struggling to keep our heads above water, did all she knew to keep Barb as comfortable as possible. A neighbor friend invited Mom to church with these words, "If you bring your baby to church, God will heal her." (Side note: I love and trust God but cannot personally imagine being so bold or confident to promise this, just sayin'.) Mom was at the end of her rope, so she consented. After the singing and preaching, as the service

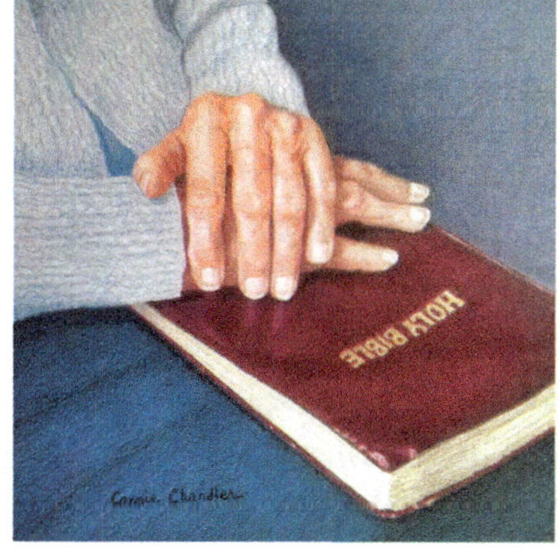

was closing, our neighbor came and took Barb from Mom's arms. She walked to the front and asked the pastor to pray for her, which he did. The next morning every scab and sore was gone except for a small one in Barb's very chubby elbow crease. That evening Mom vowed, "Any God who would love my baby this much, I will serve for the rest of my life." And she has.

Mom passed away at the age of ninety-one. She walked with God, sought to know Him through prayer and reading the Bible, and prayed for us and our families every day of her life. Mom was faithful to God, faithful to her family, and faithful to her friends. She has modeled love and steadfastness to us throughout our lives. I am deeply grateful for the legacy Mom has given our family.

A few years ago, my sister Connie, an artist, asked for a picture of Mom's hands placed on her Bible. This snapshot is Connie's picture of Mom's hands and the faith that guided her throughout her life. For Connie, Barb, Jeni and me, it expresses a deep foundational gratitude. We have weathered some tough seasons yet are still close and committed to one another, and deeply grateful for Mom's love and perseverance.

Families can be challenging. We are born or brought into a group of people who shape, embrace, and sometimes wound us. It seems easier to walk away sometimes than to work through things. Every family system is unique; I do not presume to lay a template over how each of us should respond within our family. I simply want to encourage you to take a moment and be grateful for what God has given through your family—without ifs, ands, or buts. It's not a scale where we balance the good against the bad and decide whether there is enough good to make us grateful. Rather, for whatever good that is there, be thankful. For the fact that you have life today, be thankful. And if there is a situation that requires forgiveness or conversation, do it.

There is a lot of chaos, pain, and darkness in this upside-down world of ours, but my prayer is that you would see the goodness of God in your life. Whether it's in the faces of the people you love, the resources that make your life comfortable, or the beauty of the world around you, take a few moments and say *Thank You* to the One who gives so freely. Perhaps this snapshot of one woman's faithful loving hands will give you peace and hope.

Further Reading

Philippians 1:3 *Every time I think of you, I give thanks to my God.*

Philippians 4:6 *Don't worry about anything; instead, pray about everything. Tell God what you need, and thank him for all he has done.*

Psalm 100 *Shout with joy to the Lord, all the earth! Worship the Lord with gladness. Come before him, singing with joy. Acknowledge that the Lord is God! He made us, and we are his. We are his people, the sheep of his pasture. Enter his gates with thanksgiving; go into his courts with praise. Give thanks to him and praise his name. For the Lord is good. His unfailing love continues forever, and his faithfulness continues to each generation.*

I have met people over the years who looked to be deeply grounded, wise and strong—the kind of people on whom you could lean and depend, who could weather the stuff of life. I've also known people who seemed fragile and breakable yet found them to be incredibly resilient. Ultimately, it seems, you cannot always tell from outward appearance how deep and strong one's root system goes.

I sat with a woman who had lost a child, and I could not fathom how she would make it through the day. Yet, as weeks, months, and years passed, she found strength, found her way. I talked with a man whose wife left him, and he had become emotionally debilitated, losing his ability to connect with his children or friends. He never recovered, becoming more bitter and utterly unhappy. Often it is a matter of grounding or roots. I have not yet found a way to avoid the pains of life, but I have seen incredible nobility in people in the face of severe struggles. There is something in their root system that determines how they will fare in the face of adversity.

My mom, as I've noted before, was a single mother, poor as could be, who worked two jobs to feed her three girls. With a controlling and abusive father, and an alcoholic, absent husband, how in the world could she survive? If you knew my mom later in life you would not assume her hardships. She was a kind, peaceful woman who loved easily. How does that happen? She had a *very* strong root system. Part of it came from her mother who was a beautiful soul living in wretched conditions with grace, but faith was the greatest part of Mom's root system. She would tell you that her faith gave her the strength to endure anything. It was also the means by which she saw good in most things and people.

There is a ninety-nine-point-nine percent chance that you have faced some very difficult "stuff" in your life. You may be facing it right now. How are you holding up? How is your root system? I encourage you to choose forgiveness, kindness, grace and love, rather than anger, resentment, and bitterness. Develop a deep and steady root system through faithfulness, integrity, and character. Choose to live a generous and honest life.

Like Mom, my roots are also grounded deeply in faith. Faith in the goodness and love of God is the surest foundation you can have. He is all the courage and hope you'll need in even the greatest storms. What are you facing today? Where do you need strength? I pray that you will discover your deep, steadfast roots and there find the peace and strength you need in your life.

Further Reading

Isaiah 41:10 *Don't be afraid, for I am with you. Don't be discouraged, for I am your God. I will strengthen you and help you. I will hold you up with my victorious right hand.*

Isaiah 40:31 *But those who trust in the Lord will find new strength. They will soar high on wings like eagles. They will run and not grow weary. They will walk and not faint.*

Galatians 6:9 *So let's not get tired of doing what is good. At just the right time we will reap a harvest of blessing if we don't give up.*

2 Corinthians 12:9 *Each time he said, "My grace is all you need. My power works best in weakness." So now I am glad to boast about my weaknesses, so that the power of Christ can work through me.*

Proverbs 20:7 *The godly walk with integrity; blessed are their children who follow them.*

Hebrews 12:1 *Therefore, since we are surrounded by such a huge crowd of witnesses to the life of faith, let us strip off every weight that slows us down, especially the sin that so easily trips us up. And let us run with endurance the race God has set before us.*

[Choices, Faithfulness, Guidance, Self-Control]

Chapter 37

A Snapshot of....

HUMBLE HANDS

Are you humble? Do you want to be? Before you answer, we should probably define the word. What does it mean to be humble?

Humility is a state of mind that is reflected in the way we see and respond to every other human being. It comes from the Latin *humilis,* meaning lowliness of mind, modesty, unpretentiousness. It can also mean a low opinion of oneself. To whom do you feel just a bit superior by wealth, race, religion, gender or ethnicity? To whom do you feel inferior by the same criteria? Either way, that's the wrong kind of thinking. The truth is, we are all broken in ways, strange and needy in ways. The truth is also that we are wonderfully and beautifully created and are part of the colorful tapestry of humanity. Humility embraces the value in others and in ourselves.

In this snapshot we see the well-manicured hands of a woman washing the dirty, worn feet of a man. Reverse their roles and it is the same message. Insert a Republican and a Democrat, a light, medium or darker-skinned person, a wealthy and a poor person, a Muslim and a Christian, or any who hold differing opinions or status. I know washing someone's feet is not something we do much these days, but it symbolizes an attitude that is willing to serve others, especially those who are different from us.

How do we live humbly? It is not through comparison or competition. And it's not about surrendering to oppression or abuse. It is the basic truth that you and others are made by the same God. We are all flawed and we are all valuable. Imagine a world where people chose to serve others first and allowed themselves to be served, honoring our joint humanity. In *Mere Christianity*, C.S. Lewis writes, "As long as you are proud you cannot know God. A proud man is always looking down on things and people: and, of course, as long as you are looking down you cannot see something that is above you."

We may want to grow in humility but need to remember that it doesn't just happen. It is a choice we make for the sake of our best life, made possible by the grace of God. Humility is also *foundational* to our identity. When someone compliments me on a lesson, sermon, or such, I could respond, "It's all God. I'm nothing. I'm scum." But If I really understand God is good and made me for a purpose then I can truthfully say, "Thank you! I'm so grateful for your kind words and that my teaching helped in some way." I know I'm neither scum nor divine. I'm just hanging out in my place of grace.

There has never been a greater picture of humility than what we see in Philippians 2:5-11, included below. God Himself chose to become a man and live a poor and ultimately fatal human existence. Jesus, the Son of God, *chose* to lower Himself and suffer as a human. Never did this mean He was insignificant or worthless. Quite the contrary, He was God on a mission. And God's mission has offered us life and hope. We get to choose.

Who, today, could you serve or help? Even as you consider that question, is there someone you refuse to help, whether because you know them too well, or because they are different? Are you willing to shift your thinking in order to humbly serve someone else? I pray so.

Further Reading

Phil 2:5-11 *Your attitude should be the same that Christ Jesus had. Though he was God he did not demand and cling to his rights as God.* ***He made himself*** *nothing;* ***he took the humble position*** *of a slave and appeared in human form. And in human form he obediently* ***humbled himself*** *even further by dying a criminal's death on a cross. Because of this, God raised him up to the heights of heaven and gave him a name that is above every other name, so that at the name of Jesus every knee will bow, in heaven and on earth and under the earth, and every tongue will* *confess that Jesus Christ is Lord, to the glory of God the Father.* [emphasis mine]

2 Corinthians 8:9 *You know how full of love and kindness our Lord Jesus Christ was. Though he was very rich, yet for your sakes he became poor, so that by his poverty he could make you rich.*

Matthew 23:11,12 *The greatest among you must be a servant. But those who exalt themselves will be humbled, and those who humble themselves will be exalted.*

Matthew 11:28,29 *Then Jesus said, "Come to me, all of you who are weary and carry heavy burdens, and I will give you rest. Take my yoke upon you. Let me teach you because I am humble and gentle, and you will find rest for your souls. For my yoke fits perfectly, and the burden I give you is light."*

Micah 6:8 *No, O people, the Lord has already told you what is good, and this is what he requires: to do what is right, to love mercy, and to walk humbly with your God.*

[Choices, Humility, Relationships, Serving]

Chapter 38

A Snapshot of….

BINOS AND PERSPECTIVE

When my kids were young, I would take them out of school for opening day at Dodger Stadium. It was a tradition for us. I bought a legit scorebook from a sporting goods store and my son and I kept a running detailed scoresheet.

Since we didn't have front row seats (far from it, literally) my kids and I would use our excellent binoculars to see the individual players. I loved being able to see their faces. They weren't just small faceless figures playing baseball like wind-up toys, they were our heroes—we were big Dodger fans. We would pass the binoculars back and forth, feeling like a part of what was going on down on the field. Sometimes, one of us would accidently look through the wrong end of the glasses, resulting in making the field and players appear incredibly tiny and farther away. Not the result we were going for. The downside, though, was you couldn't see the game—the big picture—when focused on just one thing.

Many times in life I've missed the bigger picture because I was so focused on just one thing. When Budd and I were struggling in our marriage I was so focused on my unhappiness that I missed how hard he worked, how much he loved me and the kids, and how much I was contributing to our distance. During the times when we lived paycheck to paycheck, I was so focused on being poor and not having enough that I failed to notice that we had all we needed, including our home.

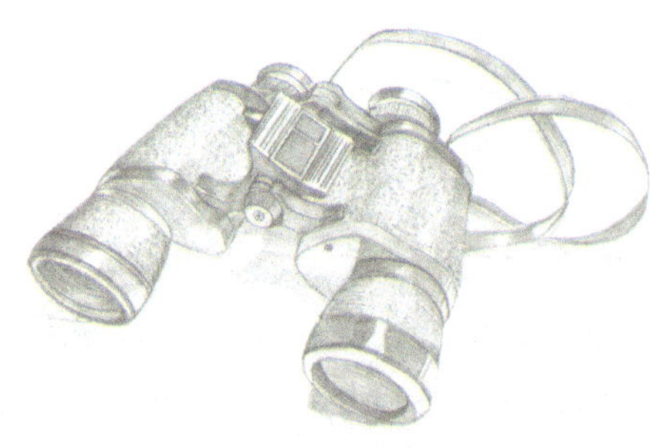

We humans can get very bogged down focusing on the wrong things. Our interior binoculars cause us to focus too closely on minor things and miss the major things. We look at our life through binoculars that either make things look bigger than they really are, or smaller.

It is important to occasionally take the time and effort to pause and look at your life. Is what you are prioritizing most important? Are people higher on your list than things? Do you ever look at your calendar or finances to see if they reflect what you value most? It's one thing to say that your family is your priority, but do they get quality time? Do you profess to love God but He gets neither your time nor your attention?

With the constant barrage of information, challenges, and demands on your life it is easy to get caught up in the tyranny of the urgent (and too often it's what someone else says is urgent).

Now is a good time to pause, exhale, and adjust your binoculars to focus on what is most important. If you aren't sure what that is, ask God. He knows it all.

The Bible addresses this issue of flipped priorities a lot. We are cautioned against making money and stuff our chief priority because it does not last and it won't give us life. We are told that busyness without rest will pretty much kill us—if not our body, definitely our soul. If we focus on what others think of us rather than on our character, we will waste relationships and diminish our influence.

There are thousands of books that tell us who we should be and how we should live. I'm not suggesting you become a self-help addict and ingest all that information. I believe your very best decision is to go to the One who created you. Don't just ask the question, "What is most important in my life and what should I do?" but take the time to hang out with God. Read what the Bible says about how you were created and what matters most for your best life.

Is this easy? I don't always think so. We're distracted by what's around us and want mostly to satisfy our wants and avoid discomfort. That's not always bad, it's just not the most important thing. People who love me have sacrificed for my good. I have done the same for others at times. Yet even when I pray, I find that many of my prayers are geared to my comfort, even if they sound like they're for others. "Lord, please find them a job," so I don't have to keep worrying. "Lord, please heal them," so I don't have to keep helping them. It sounds awful when I put it into words, but that doesn't change the reality of my tainted heart.

Perhaps you echo my prayer: Lord, I truly do want to be a person who knows and lives by your priorities. How can I lose when what you want most is for me to live my best life and to make a difference on my corner of this planet? God, help me adjust my binoculars to see as you see. Thank you. Amen.

Further Reading

Matthew 6:33-34 NTE *Instead, make your top priority God's kingdom and his way of life, and all these things will be given to you as well. 'So don't worry about tomorrow. Tomorrow can worry about itself. One day's trouble at a time is quite enough.'*

2 Chronicles 26:1-5 *All the people of Judah had crowned Amaziah's sixteen-year-old son, Uzziah, as king in place of his father. After his father's death, Uzziah rebuilt the town of Elath and restored it to Judah. Uzziah was sixteen years old when he became king, and he reigned in Jerusalem fifty-two years. His mother was Jecoliah from Jerusalem. He did what was pleasing in the LORD's sight, just as his father, Amaziah, had done. Uzziah sought God during the days of Zechariah, who taught him to fear God. And as long as the king sought guidance from the LORD, God gave him success.* (Young King Uzziah had to keep his binoculars focused on God.)

James 1:2-6 *Dear brothers and sisters, when troubles of any kind come your way, consider it an opportunity for great joy. For you know that when your faith is tested, your endurance has a* *chance to grow. So let it grow, for when your endurance is fully developed, you will be perfect and complete, needing nothing. If you need wisdom, ask our generous God, and he will give it to you. He will not rebuke you for asking. But when you ask him, be sure that your faith is in God alone. Do not waver, for a person with divided loyalty is as unsettled as a wave of the sea that is blown and tossed by the wind.*

[Choices, Perspective]

Chapter 39

A Snapshot of....

SLOWLY DYING IVY

Budd and I celebrated our thirty-ninth wedding anniversary with deep gratitude for all God had done in us and for us. As we talked about our big fortieth the following year, we planned a trip to New England, something we had dreamed of doing since we lived in Boston during Budd's Army days. We both loved the idea and Budd enjoyed planning it all.

Two weeks later, on July 10, Budd died in his sleep. We had played golf that day then shopped for supplies for a 'Low Country Boil' he was fixing for dinner guests that night. It was a great day. For some reason, I was patient and helpful (not always my go-to attitude with Budd's projects). It was a really,

really, good day. As usual, I went to bed a couple of hours before Budd, the night owl. At 2:40 a.m. I woke up because Budd was snoring unusually loudly. I nudged him to get him to roll onto his side, but he was already on his side. I couldn't wake him up. I called the paramedics. Budd was gone, just like that.

Up to this point, I had experienced death as an event—one massive loss. And it is, but with Budd's death I also experienced an ongoing loss. I anticipated it would be like an explosion where I would get hurt, but then just wait until the wounds healed. There is some of that, but I wasn't prepared for the first time someone from his past called to say hi and I had to tell them he had died. September twenty-first was my mom's birthday. She lived with us, and she and Budd were close. On her birthday it was fresh again. October ninth was my birthday, the sixteenth our daughter's. Then came Thanksgiving, then Christmas, and on it went. Birthdays, holidays, experiences: rather than an explosion, losing Budd was like an ivy plant that has died at the root, but the leaves haven't withered yet. You see a green ivy leaf and expect it to be alive, but it isn't. The memory of Budd's involvement in just about every facet of my life gave the impression that he would show up in some way for all of it, but he didn't. In the day-to-day stuff I got used to it, but on those special occasions it would throw me again.

Once I embraced this reality, I found that I could look for that ivy leaf and let it touch me with a gentle grief, but also a deep appreciation for who Budd was. He loved me very much and took care of our family well. He was funny, tender, smart, and sometimes a pain in the neck. All of that was a life that grew intertwined with mine, and when he died it was a slow unwinding of our two selves. I have a good life today. My kids and grandkids are wonderful. Because of Budd's wise planning, I am comfortable in my life. I have had to learn a lot of new things over the last years, but it's been doable.

Grief is a very personal journey. I've learned to give myself and others permission to find their own way. I have faced other losses that are not as dramatic as death, and I find that allowing for grief and time is still the best way to walk. Avoiding grief doesn't work. Let it come, let it touch you and let it pass.

I no longer pine for Budd. When the family gets together, we often laugh and tell 'Budd stories.' It is not melancholy, it is family. We still encounter milestones where his absence is noticeable—like when our latest granddaughter was born or our grandsons graduated high school, then college. Budd loved being a grandpa. But seldom do ivy leaves crop up anymore. The grief and pain are gone, but occasionally I'm aware of loneliness. And a deep appreciation for the life of someone I loved and who loved me, a man with whom I built a solid life of faith and family.

The Bible is filled with stories of loss and grief. We're never told to ignore it, nor are we told to set up housekeeping there. "In this world you'll face trouble," Jesus said and He was right. I've talked with people who turned their back on God because He didn't spare them pain and loss. That seems an illogical response to me; sadness, loss and grief are going to happen to all of us at some point. Why would we choose to navigate those times alone? God promises to be with us through all of it.

My life has held its share of struggle and sadness but certainly not worse than most people I know. In every single case God showed himself compassionate, merciful, and wise. God has been faithful to me and to my family. My church community has walked every step with us, too. It is always a choice to face life with God and others or to go it alone. For me, it's no longer something I wrestle with; He is the only way to life, peace, and hope. It's just a fact. May the God of peace be your traveling companion in life, too. Invite Him.

Further Reading

Psalm 34:18 *The LORD is close to the brokenhearted; he rescues those whose spirits are crushed.*

John 16:33 *"I have told you all this so that you may have peace in me. Here on earth you will have many trials and sorrows. But take heart, because I have overcome the world."*

Revelation 3:2 *"Look! I stand at the door and knock. If you hear my voice and open the door, I will come in, and we will share a meal together as friends."*

Psalm 145:18 *The LORD is close to all who call on him, yes, to all who call on him in truth.*

Acts 17:27 *His purpose was for the nations to seek after God and perhaps feel their way toward him and find him—though he is not far from any one of us.*

Isaiah 43:2 *When you go through deep waters, I will be with you. When you go through rivers of difficulty, you will not drown.*

When you walk through the fire of oppression, you will not be burned up; the flames will not consume you.

[Grief, Support, Trust]

Chapter 40

A Snapshot of....

An Unprotected House

I've never been great with boundaries. I may have plans to do something, or to not do anything, and a request comes to me and I usually say, "Okay," whether I want to do it or not. I'm better than I used to be, but I wouldn't call it a strength.

Several years ago, I was approaching burnout. As a pastor and a counselor, I had come to believe that I should be absolutely available to anyone, anytime. My family, of course, got the short end of the stick with my time and attention. But how could they not see I was helping people? The last person on my list of priorities was me: personal time, self-care, or a minute to think were never on the day's agenda.

One day, as I literally felt like I was losing my mental balance, I saw in my mind's eye a little yellow house set on rolling green hills. It was a sweet house, but all the doors and windows were open, and animals, birds, leaves, and dust were free to blow through every corner. The inside of the little house was filled with all the things animals and nature leave in their wake. As so often happens, I heard God speak to my heart through that picture: "Kathy, it's okay to close the doors and windows sometimes and to enjoy the peace, quiet, and privacy of your home. It's good for you to bring order to your home and to fill it with peace for you and your family. Close the doors. Close the windows. Exhale."

And so, I did. The house represented both my literal home and my daily life. I began to set times when I was not available, sometimes because I didn't feel like it and sometimes because I wanted to have time alone with my family or myself. It was difficult to set those boundaries, but it got easier. The feeling of freedom I experienced and the wonderful times with my family made it all worth it. I began to regain my footing.

We live in a place and an age of constant activity, always something to do. We have information badgering us from every angle, needs from every direction, and FOMO (Fear of Missing Out) for many. What if we said *no* to some things? Perhaps you don't need to close your house, but what about putting some boundaries on your mind and heart? What if you didn't spend hours on devices, watching or listening to others talking on podcasts, radio, and TV? Take the opportunity to practice peace, to acclimate to quiet and get re-acquainted with yourself. It's not just about being alone, it's about being renewed and restored through peace. For me, this has always and only come about through God's love and grace. That's my anchor.

I grew up in chaos: alcoholism, abuse, poverty. From about the age of four, we attended a small local church where Mom was introduced to God's love and goodness. I have a strong legacy of faith, but I have not always lived in the peace that the Bible promises. Fear and insecurity marked my childhood and early adult years. I prayed a lot for peace of mind and heart, but it was not forthcoming. Raising my kids, working at marriage, and dealing with my own interior issues led me to crave peace. I wanted my kids to learn to live in peace, and that wasn't going to happen if I didn't go after it myself.

It has been quite a process, but I can honestly say that I am learning to like myself more and to appreciate time spent with… me. My brain is a strange and magical place that I have had to learn to accept. Seriously, I have some really weird thoughts at times, but I no longer run from my reality or my imagination. I'm learning to live with time in my "house" alone, which is really time alone with God. He is the peacemaker and offers me the grace I need to accept my weirdness.

Even Jesus, who is God Himself, found it necessary to get away by Himself when He walked the earth. He worked hard at loving, healing, and teaching people and He needed rest and quiet. I figure if God needed to exhale (check out Genesis, chapter one) it is ridiculous to think I can overlook it.

For those of you who find it difficult to quiet your mind and close your doors, I encourage you to learn from my rough journey. Don't wait until you're almost losing it. Find a rhythm of social life and private life, of listening to the world around you and of listening to the voice of peace inside you.

Further Reading

Psalm 4:8 *In peace I will lie down and sleep, for you alone, O LORD, will keep me safe.*

Psalm 29:11 *The LORD gives his people strength. The LORD blesses them with peace.*

Matthew 14:23 *After sending them home, he went up into the hills by himself to pray. Night fell while he was there alone.*

Mark 6:31 *Then Jesus said, "Let's go off by ourselves to a quiet place and rest awhile." He said this because there were so many people coming and going that Jesus and his apostles didn't even have time to eat.*

Galatians 5:22-23 *But the Holy Spirit produces this kind of fruit in our lives: love, joy, peace, patience, kindness, goodness, faithfulness, gentleness, and self-control. There is no law against these things!*

[Choices, Peace, Rest]

Chapter 41

A Snapshot of....

DISAPPOINTMENT

When Budd was studying for his driver's exam he asked his dad, "May I have a car for my birthday?" "Sure," came the ready reply. As Budd tells it, the morning of his sixteenth birthday he awoke with an anticipation that was unprecedented. He raced downstairs and out the front door. Seeing only the family station wagon, he raced to the side of the house. Nothing. He ran back into the house where his parents were having their morning coffee.

"Where's the car?"

"What car?"

"You said I could have a car for my birthday!"

"And you can. You just need to buy one."

Now, this exchange can make you think my father-in-law was cruel. He truly was not. He had grown up working to support himself since he was very young. He was a hard worker and good provider. This was a lesson for his eldest son. While Budd told the story often with a tinge of humor, there was also the faint scent of the disappointment he had felt so many years before. Big expectation equals big disappointment. Large or small, important or not, I hate being disappointed.

Disappointment is the result of an expectation that doesn't work out. By definition it is "to fail to fulfill the expectation or hope of." When I expect someone to do something and they don't, I'm disappointed. When I expect a gadget, appliance, or car to function a certain way and it doesn't, I'm disappointed. These disappointments are just a way of life. My granddaughter is disappointed to tears when she can't have a cake pop. Life is not easy.

Some disappointments are life-altering. I have a friend whose pregnancy was a gift of joy and expectation. She and her husband were ecstatic, as most soon-to-be-parents are. Their baby girl was born and lived mere hours. *Disappointment* is almost too small a word for their grief. They expected so much more, so much different. Their journey would take days, months, and years dealing with that sad disappointment.

When a couple in love gets married, their expectation is that they will be happy and build a life together. Few people believe it will be perfect or even easy, but there is still the expectation that they will be able to make it work. Divorce can be a crushing disappointment. Even if the divorce seems necessary, it is still the death of what could have been. I know of graduates who have studied for years to pursue a career that does not work out; the hope of parents that their children will return and reconcile but never do. So much sadness and disappointment.

The truth is, I am usually most disappointed in myself; disappointed that I wasn't or am not a perfect mother, grandmother, or friend with the ability to love perfectly, have the wisdom and resources my kids need every single time they need it, and never respond in anger, frustration, or self-centeredness. That's all I want. I can't be perfect, but I'd like to be better.

Sometimes we are disappointed in others. Why don't people appreciate our obvious gifts and abilities? Why do friends sometimes hurt or disappoint us? How can friends confront us just because we mess up a little? Where's the grace?

We can even be disappointed in God. He didn't come through, He didn't listen, He didn't heal, He is silent. All of these conclusions are based on the expectations of who God is and how He should act. Not surprisingly, He usually does not mold Himself to suit our expectations. We read certain Scriptures and form certain expectations, such as:

> "*My God will supply all your needs according to his riches in glory.*" (Phil 4:13) I need a new roof on my house. Where is that coming from? I need a job, or financial help.
>
> "*God will not allow you to be tempted more than you're able to bear.*" (1 Cor 10:13) Well, I can't take anymore. God isn't coming through like He said He was. I'm on my own.

> "*By his stripes we are healed.*" (Isa 53:5) "*The prayer of faith will heal the sick.*" (James 5:15) I have prayed with all the faith I can muster. I have trusted and tried and wept and pleaded with God and, nothing. I am sometimes disappointed in God.

When God came to earth—some people were disappointed. The prophets had promised big things! Deliverance and freedom! And people expected a mighty warrior king! Jesus, the very Son of God, came as a baby. He never took on the political power they anticipated. It's still true, right? He just doesn't perform for us, or do things our way.

Why are we so disappointed in God and in ourselves? I believe it's because we expect too much or the wrong things. We expect God to act a certain way based on our limited understanding.

God, the Creator of all things is "Other" than us, not just a shinier version of us. He is magnificently above everything even as He is lovingly present with us. Wrap your brain around that if you can. We cannot earn, purchase, or require His goodness toward us, it is a gift He is delighted to give. God's ways, His plans, and His presence will always hold mystery for us. His ways and thoughts are so very different from ours, as Isaiah writes in the passage below.

When life feels out of control, lean into Him. He doesn't move or change. When you are disappointed in life or in God, tell Him. He can take it. When you are suffering, reach out to God and know with absolute assurance that He is close, He cares and He will use our pain to work goodness and grace in us. I know that doesn't sound as good as having a Great-Genie-in-the-Sky who is at our beck and call, but then our purpose in life is so much greater than we can imagine.

Expect God to love you. Expect life to be hard sometimes. Expect His ultimate good for those who love Him. Expect Him to offer grace to you. You won't be disappointed.

Further Reading

Isaiah 55:8-9 *"My thoughts are nothing like your thoughts," says the Lord. "And my ways are far beyond anything you could imagine. For just as the heavens are higher than the earth, so my ways are higher than your way and my thoughts higher than your thoughts."*

Exodus 15:11 *Who is like you among the gods, O LORD— glorious in holiness, awesome in splendor, performing great wonders?*

Psalm 40:5 *O LORD my God, you have performed many wonders for us. Your plans for us are too numerous to list. You have no equal. If I tried to recite all your wonderful deeds, I would never come to the end of them.*

Psalm 143:11 *For the glory of your name, O LORD, preserve my life. Because of your faithfulness, bring me out of this distress.*

Matthew 9:22 *Jesus turned around, and when he saw her he said, "Daughter, be encouraged! Your faith has made you well." And the woman was healed at that moment.*

Psalm 139:17 *How precious are your thoughts about me, O God. They cannot be numbered!*

[God's Character, Pain, Perspective, Trust]

Chapter 42

A Snapshot of....

A Desperate Grasp

I have a very dear friend who battled aggressive cancer, more than once. She was one of the dearest and sweetest people I know. Her family and friends loved her and demonstrated that love through their time, money, food, prayers, and labor on her behalf—everything from cleaning the house to caring for her ailing body. These are the kind of friends who would not give up even when this ugly disease kept taking more territory.

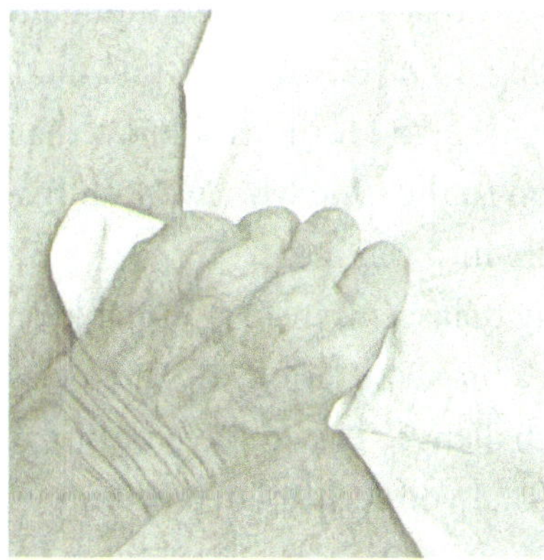

As I was praying for her one day, I saw a picture in my mind: her hand held tightly to the hem of a garment, certainly inspired by the story in the Bible of the ailing woman who sought healing from Jesus by grabbing the hem of His robe (Matt 9:20-22). The message, I knew, was that so often all we really have is the ability to hold on. Especially for my friend, this picture seemed to represent a narrowed focus on what she *could* do. There was no new medication or treatment to consider, no demands she could have made, or special soup that would fix everything. Her life situation brought a laser focus on what mattered most: her love for Jesus, her earnest and deep faith in God. She talked to Him as though she could see Him right in the room with her (which just may be true for her). She knew Jesus.

She spent her days, her minutes, coping with pain and the ravages of this awful disease, with little to no power over her circumstances. But she had the grip of a giant when it came to holding onto Jesus. When I shared this snapshot with her, she said it was exactly what she was feeling and needed. And so, every day when I'd think of her, love her, and pray for her, I held onto the same hem she was clinging to. God and God alone had her life in the palm of His hand.

I am not saying that if she had held tightly enough God would have healed her. We don't control God, and I don't believe He requires us to earn His goodness by our efforts. I know that He is good and can do anything. I also know that His ways and thoughts are beyond our human understanding. I prayed earnestly that God would heal my dear friend. But even though He didn't, I know that her grip did not falter as she held on to the One who was holding onto her as she passed from this life into the next.

I don't know what you face today that seems insurmountable or utterly overwhelming. Perhaps it is a broken relationship, financial issues, job problems or a health challenge. It may be emotional or psychological challenges that make you feel isolated or bound up. Whatever it is, there is always one thing you can do that truly matters. Hold on to the One who holds onto you.

Further Reading

Check out Lauren Daigle singing "Hold On To Me" on YouTube. The lyrics are amazing.

Matthew 9:20-22 *Just then a woman who had suffered for twelve years with constant bleeding came up behind him. She touched the fringe of his robe, for she thought, "If I can just touch his robe, I will be healed." Jesus turned around, and when he saw her he said, "Daughter, be encouraged! Your faith has made you well." And the woman was healed at that moment.*

Isaiah 55:8-9 *"My thoughts are nothing like your thoughts," says the LORD. "And my ways are far beyond anything you could imagine. For just as the heavens are higher than the earth, so my ways are higher than your ways and my thoughts higher than your thoughts."*

Romans 8:35, 37-39 *Can anything ever separate us from Christ's love? Does it mean he no longer loves us if we have trouble or calamity, or are persecuted, or hungry, or destitute, or in danger, or threatened with death? No, despite all these things, overwhelming victory is ours through Christ, who loved us. And I am convinced that nothing can ever separate us from God's love. Neither death nor life, neither angels nor demons, neither* *our fears for today nor our worries about tomorrow—not even the powers of hell can separate us from God's love. No power in the sky above or in the earth below—indeed, nothing in all creation will ever be able to separate us from the love of God that is revealed in Christ Jesus our Lord.*

[Despair, Faith, Hope, Perseverance]

Chapter 43

A Snapshot of....

A USELESS SEPTIC TANK

Seven of us stood in a loose circle around the dark hole. My friends were finally hooked up to city sewage and now had to deal with the septic tank buried in their back yard. The guys had dug down a couple of feet to the clay tank then had broken through to reveal the wet, dark, cavernous tank. It was not a pleasant sight or smell, but we were going to fill that puppy up and we'd be good to go. There was a mound of dirt near the hole but we quickly realized that it could not fill the massive space inside. Then, a brilliant idea! We would toss in a bunch of junk from their garage—old bicycles, an old camping cooler, even a few broken chairs. The idea was to fill up the space with junk and finish it off with dirt before replacing the topsoil. Is that a great idea or what?

It wasn't that easy. At one point, my friend accidently dropped the javelin-like pole used to break apart the clay tank into the hole. This required a ladder, a descent into the pit and a retrieval.

Difficult, smelly business for sure. What seemed like a whole lot of big stuff filled it less than anticipated. The rest of us went to get our castoffs, and for a few hours we gathered and tossed junk into the dark hole, then added dirt. Then more dirt. Still no sign of filling. Finally, it was agreed that much more dirt was required. Lots of it. Ultimately, the hole was filled, the ground restored and grass seeded. It took so much more than our initial solution anticipated.

This septic adventure is a cautionary tale about how we fill the gaps, holes, and empty places in our life. Whether from childhood wounds, destructive patterns as adults, dissolved marriages and families, or a multitude of other issues, life can hollow us out, destabilize our foundation and turn septic. As we grow into adulthood, we may not be fully aware of the hollow dark places until we find ourselves trying to fill up our need for love, acceptance, and security with all the wrong things—food, sex, alcohol, drugs, anger, and hiding, and more. The problem is that none of those things work beyond the immediate gratification. We may feel

better for a minute but that doesn't mean it will hold. Too often the unhappiness, dissatisfaction, and pain grow exponentially with every attempt to cover it. What's a body to do?

First, find out what the hole is and you'll know better how to fill it. My childhood trauma from poverty, abuse, and divorce resulted in an adulthood with great insecurities and a deep, deep need to be loved and accepted. I tried to fill that hole with food and with "good girl syndrome"—doing everything I could to keep everyone around me happy and liking me. I never learned to identify or verbalize my own needs, there wasn't room for that when I was so desperate to be accepted. The result of these unhealthy patterns was that my body grew in girth while my soul withered. That is not the way to a good life.

Only by God's kindness and grace did I come to understand and trust that I was worth caring for and that my needs were as important as yours. All of the things I'd used over the years to fill that empty tank were useless, but as I surrendered to God's loving kindness, He began to fill in the dark, lonely, scarred places with light and love. It really did change everything for me. I am not all I want to be, yet, but I have come to like and appreciate my "unique" self. (Some would use the word strange. I prefer unique.)

My invitation to you, dear reader, is to go after the septic areas of your life and begin to fill them with what gives real life. Whether you begin with prayer, talking with friends who know you, therapy, or reading helpful books, start somewhere. My personal belief is that the best and only truly successful path is to move toward the One who created you, knows you, and loves you more than you can imagine. He wants only goodness for you and He is enough to fill every single cavernous hole. It's true. I know it.

Further Reading

Ezekiel 36:26 *And I will give you a new heart, and I will put a new spirit in you. I will take out your stony, stubborn heart and give you a tender, responsive heart.*

Romans 12:1-2 *And so, dear brothers and sisters, I plead with you to give your bodies to God because of all he has done for you. Let them be a living and holy sacrifice—the kind he will find acceptable. This is truly the way to worship him. Don't copy the behavior and customs of this world, but let God transform you into a new person by changing the way you think. Then you will learn to know God's will for you, which is good and pleasing and perfect.*

Psalm 51:10 *Create in me a clean heart, O God. Renew a loyal spirit within me.*

Isaiah 40:31 *But those who trust in the LORD will find new strength. They will soar high on wings like eagles. They will run and not grow weary. They will walk and not faint.*

Jeremiah 31:3 *Long ago the LORD said to Israel: "I have loved you, my people, with an everlasting love. With unfailing love I have drawn you to myself."*

[Choices, Habits, Restoration, Self-Care]

Chapter 44

A Snapshot of....

STANDING FIRM

Years ago, I entered a grocery store that had a giant scale in the lobby area. It was one of those you step on and the needle on the giant scale in front of your face boldly races in a circle like clock hands, refusing to stop, climbing, climbing, ever climbing. Did I step up on that scale when I entered the store? *No!* Why? Well, possibly because I don't weigh one-hundred-and-ten pounds, and possibly because it's no one's business how much I weigh!

But here's the thing: whether it's displayed on a giant public scale, at home for my eyes only, or simply avoided all together, it doesn't change what I weigh. Not looking at it or not allowing others to see it doesn't make the reality go away. I am not smaller or lighter simply because I don't know that number. In fact, not knowing the truth of my weight makes it much more likely that I will increase that number. Ignoring the truth is harmful, not helpful.

While the concept of owning the truth of our weight or age is easily understood, the broader question is, Are we living in truth? What is the core truth of your life that is unchanging? Do you even have such a truth? I'm not talking about truth as opposed to a lie, but rather something that is true like a plumb line or ruler. It is a deep-seated, unswerving, and foundational truth that grounds us, holds us steady and directs our daily life. It can be that you believe human life is sacred, faithfulness to your spouse, or that kindness is part of your rule of life. Whatever it is, your understanding of truth guides how you treat others and yourself.

Over the years I have found myself in situations that were confusing and unsettling. I didn't know what to do, how to feel, which way to turn or how to proceed. When this happens, I pause, close my eyes, and picture my feet on a rock. There may be chaotic thoughts and emotions swirling around me, but my feet are steady on the rock. This picture helps me in seasons of uncertainty and reminds me who I am.

The rock for me is God and His truth. There is so much in life that keeps changing and shifting with uncertainty—relationships, finances, jobs, politics, health and so much more, can slowly or radically change. Where do you stand when your foundation is shaken? I have found only one thing, one Person, strong enough to hold me and all of my stuff.

Take this quick quiz. True or False:

— The earth is flat.

— The sun revolves around the earth.

— The earth was created in 4004 BC.

— A deck of playing cards is evil.

— Dancing is a vertical expression of a horizontal desire.

At one time all these statements were considered true, by someone. We know now that the earth is round and revolves around the sun. Geology tells us that the earth is much older than four thousand years. Cards and dancing may not actually be the devil's playground, as asserted by my Sunday School teacher so many years ago.

When we talk about truth, we must hold loosely to some things we've been told in order to honestly pursue the truth. In hindsight, the truth can be obvious, but in the present it's tougher to see. Are there "truths" you cling to that may not really be true? Perhaps it is perceived truth about others, like, they don't like me or they are wrong, or he's a liar. We can feel something about a person or situation and allow that feeling to harden into our truth. We fail to allow people or situations to correct these potential misconceptions.

It is important that we examine our foundation. Where are my feet planted? On what am I grounded? Is it my own knowledge, another person, money, job security, or even a dream or hope? Take an honest look at what you're counting on to carry you through the stuff of life. Is it solid enough to weather political warring, relational devastation, pandemics, financial challenges, depression and anxiety? Check it out. What is under your feet today? Is it stable and strong enough to hold the weight of your life and dreams?

Further Reading

John 1:14, 16-17 *The Word became flesh and made his dwelling among us. We have seen his glory, the glory of the one and only Son, who came from the Father, full of grace and truth. Out of his fullness we have all received grace in place of grace already given. For the law was given through Moses; grace and truth came through Jesus Christ.*

John 8:32 *You'll know the truth and the truth will set you free.*

Psalm 25:5 *Guide me in your truth and teach me, for you are God my Savior, and my hope is in you all day long.*

Psalm 86:11 *Teach me your way, LORD, that I may rely on your faithfulness; give me an undivided heart, that I may fear your name.*

John 4:23 *Yet a time is coming and has now come when the true worshipers will worship the Father in the Spirit and in truth, for they are the kind of worshipers the Father seeks.*

[Choices, Truth, Wisdom]

Chapter 45

Snapshot of...

Glorious Bread

Bread. Glorious bread. Taking those bland ingredients, combining them, and creating something of such beauty, aroma, and taste. A loaf of homemade bread feels like love. Making bread is satisfying and meaningful for me.

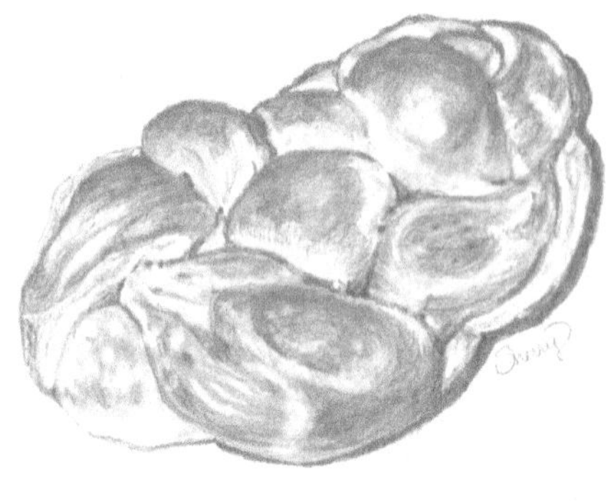

A key to good bread is kneading the dough. This is where you fold and press it over and over to break down and activate the yeast in the dough, so that when you let it rest it begins to rise, air permeating the dough. This is the difference between bread and a cracker. Kneading may not be fun for some people, but the result is nothing short of heavenly.

A friend and I had a disagreement. In the moment it was a flare-up of emotion, both of us feeling misunderstood and somewhat attacked. We talked a little and were able to, at the very least, part as friends. It took a couple of days for the harsh emotions to fade enough that I could begin to think about our disagreement—both my hurt and my hurtful words. I finally wanted to see the truth more than I wanted to be right (not an easy journey for me). When we found time to connect, I apologized and also expressed what I needed in terms of the original issue. She apologized and was able to say what she needed. The matter was settled peacefully between us.

Communication is like kneading. It may seem difficult or redundant, but it is absolutely necessary to bring life and connection between people. My friend and I had spent years practicing open and honest communication. It was what had made us good friends and it was the vital tool we needed when we had a disagreement. The result of our conversation was the aroma of peace in our relationship. The conversation, the kneading, brought the desired results.

There is another important fact about kneading bread dough: if you overdo it, you can kill the yeast. Over-kneaded dough can't be fixed and will result in a rock-hard loaf. In essence, you kill the bread's ability to rise and grow. This is equally true in relationships. Once my friend and I had settled our issue, we had to let it go. Had I brought it up again and again after we'd settled it, I could have crushed our friendship.

Too often I talk with people who live in the extremes: either the extreme of avoiding conflict by avoiding honest conversation or the extreme of saying everything that comes to mind with thin-skinned reactions. There are certainly circumstances in our lives that are hurtful and difficult to understand and to forgive. It often seems easiest to just break a relationship and avoid any difficult conversation. Truth is, though, we will not only lose relationships, we will not become the best version of ourselves. Allowing our lives to be "kneaded" means that we are willing to take the tougher road of working through misunderstandings and hurt, then let it go. If it feels almost impossible, invite a trusted third party into the conversation. We won't always understand or be understood, but we can accept one another with grace.

When I know of someone who is suffering or troubled, one of the first things I consider doing is baking a loaf of bread, not as a band-aid or pacifier, but a simple expression of love and friendship. It's one way to say, "You matter."

We need to communicate, to knead the dough. We also need to know when it's time to let it go. The Bible tells us that love covers a multitude of sins—our love for others allows us, compels us, to let go of minor annoyances and to forgive the major ones. Is there something you find you can't let go of? Is there a hurt or offense that you just keep working over and over in your mind? It's time to let it go.

May the words of my mouth and the meditation of my heart be pleasing to you, O Lord, my rock and my redeemer.
Psalm 19:14

Further Reading

Ephesians 4:2 *Always be humble and gentle. Be patient with each other, making allowance for each other's faults because of your love.*

1 Corinthians 13:4-7 *Love is patient and kind. Love is not jealous or boastful or proud or rude. It does not demand its own way. It is not irritable, and it keeps no record of being wronged. It does not rejoice about injustice but rejoices whenever the truth wins out. Love never gives up, never loses faith, is always hopeful, and endures through every circumstance.*

1 Peter 3:9 *Don't repay evil for evil. Don't retaliate with insults when people insult you. Instead, pay them back with a blessing. That is what God has called you to do, and he will grant you his blessing.*

1 Peter 4:8 *Above all, love each other deeply, because love covers over a multitude of sins.*

Proverbs 19:11 *Sensible people control their temper; they earn respect by overlooking wrongs.*

Colossians 3:13 *Make allowance for each other's faults, and forgive anyone who offends you. Remember, the Lord forgave you, so you must forgive others.*

[Communication, Forgiveness, Grace, Relationships]

Chapter 46

A Snapshot of….

A SPIDERY WEB

I watched a fly land on a spider web. It intended to take flight again but found itself stuck. The very makeup of the web held the fly's feet in place. The harder the fly worked to free itself the more stuck it became. It was mesmerizing to watch; unsettling, but mesmerizing. I know it was nature being nature, but I so desperately wanted to free the fly from the spider's web.

This is the very picture that comes to mind sometimes when I talk with people who find themselves trapped in relationship issues caused by someone else's "web." Equally, our emotional and relational brokenness can spin a web that traps others and holds them in unhealthy ways. We can be trapped by co-dependence, addiction, fear, lust, pride and so many other unlovely issues. And we can trap others with the same things. I heard a young woman once say, "I don't care why he's with me, I just want him." What a sad and ultimately destructive way to live, neither person ever feeling loved. He was trapped in her web of neediness.

How do we avoid getting caught in such a trap—or setting one? It begins with the work of knowing yourself, loving yourself, and becoming a whole person. There's an oft-quoted line from the movie, *Jerry Maguire*: "You complete me." So romantic, right? Perhaps, but it's not sound. If you need someone else in order to be a complete person you will spend your life spinning a web to trap others into filling your emptiness. It's not sustainable. Please understand that you will always be a work in progress, but you can continue to grow into a person who knows and loves yourself, and thus grow into wholeness.

In my experience it is much easier to know what we want from others than it is to discern what we truly need. When I was young, I just wanted someone to love me completely. I had so many wounds from an absent father and abusive grandfather that I wanted someone who could fill and heal those wounds. I married a man who truly loved me, but I began to resent him. Ultimately, I realized I didn't respect him because he loved *me,* a person who, at my core, didn't deserve that kind of love. By my attitude and actions, I spent too much time and energy trying to prove to him that I wasn't worthy of such love. I caught the poor man in my web of insecurity and brokenness. It took years for me to learn to love myself and to believe that:

1. God loves me just as I am.
2. I could love and accept myself as a work in progress.
3. I was love-able to others, especially my husband.

The order is important here: God, myself, others. When steps one and two are in place, even if a person rejects me, I am not utterly destroyed. They are not the love that completes me. I'm not belittling relational love. I think it is wonderful and vitally important. It just isn't *the* most vital and important. The love that keeps us free of others' webs of emotional need and co-dependence is the pure, untainted and soul-filling love of God. It is in that love that we truly become whole and complete. That's my story and I'm sticking to it.

Further Reading

Romans 12:9 *Don't just pretend to love others. Really love them. Hate what is wrong. Hold tightly to what is good.*

Ephesians 3:17-19 *Then Christ will make his home in your hearts as you trust in him. Your roots will grow down into God's love and keep you strong. And may you have the power to understand, as all God's people should, how wide, how long, how high, and how deep his love is. May you experience the love of Christ, though it is too great to understand fully. Then you will be made complete with all the fullness of life and power that comes from God.*

1 Corinthians 13:4-7 *Love is patient and kind. Love is not jealous or boastful or proud or rude. It does not demand its own way. It is not irritable, and it keeps no record of being wronged. It does not rejoice about injustice but rejoices whenever the truth wins out. Love never gives up, never loses faith, is always hopeful, and endures through every circumstance.*

Matthew 22:37-39 *Jesus replied, "'You must love the LORD your God with all your heart, all your soul, and all your mind.' This is the first and greatest commandment. A second is equally important: 'Love your neighbor as yourself.'"*

1 Peter 1:22 *You were cleansed from your sins when you obeyed the truth, so now you must show sincere love to each other as brothers and sister. Love each other deeply with all your heart.*

John 15:9 *I have loved you even as the Father has loved me. Remain in my love.*

[Brokenness, Freedom, Love, Relationships]

Chapter 47

A Snapshot of....

LISTENING HARDER

"Be quick to listen, slow to speak and slow to get angry," is one of those wise sayings from the Bible that most people nod in agreement with and believe everyone should practice. Everyone *else*, of course. In our country—inside and outside of politics, church, communities, families and friendships—there seems to be an epidemic of angry words and actions on almost every front. It appears that few are listening, all are talking, and most are angry.

So back to the verse. I may not have a solution for the masses, but I do think individually we can choose a better way and thereby make a difference. Perhaps as each of us chooses to listen longer it will begin to impact our little corner of the world. It sounds like a simple equation: listen more, talk less, and don't get angry. Why is it so difficult to do?

Having been married for thirty-nine years and raised two kids, I developed habits with my family where I assumed I knew what they would say, and I was ready with advice, correction or a sermon. (No, it was not requested by my audience.) With Budd, it was a slow learning curve to learn to listen not just to his words, but to listen for his heart and intent. Taking that time kept me from saying way too much before I even knew what the topic really was. Anger came when I began to respond without care and then he responded and then I did and on it went. Budd and I ultimately got much better at listening before we responded.

This issue played out countless times as I sat with couples in crisis, families in chaos, and friends at odds. Most often it seems that our failure to listen comes out of fear: fear of losing control, fear of being wrong, fear of having to change. Often, we fail to listen because we feel we must win to survive. Sadly, in those situations no one wins and few relationships survive.

Perhaps an important consideration is the idea of trust; that is, trusting the other person enough to let them express themselves. Understand, you don't have to agree in order to let them be heard. But I guarantee that when you do speak, you will sound kinder, wiser, and more likely to have *your* words heard and understood. Someone has to start the new pattern. Why not you?

I counseled a couple in a difficult season in their marriage. One recurring issue was his ongoing failure to call her when he was going to be home late from work. He said, "I just forgot! I was thinking about my work project and it didn't occur to me! Why is it such a big deal?" As the three of us talked, it came to this: when she was in elementary school her mother would often forget to pick her up. She would stand on the curb after everyone else was gone, beside an irritated teacher who also wanted to go home. Suddenly, the lights went on for this couple—she just wanted to know he was on his way. To their credit, they owned it and committed to do much better at communicating. It was not a huge thing to fix, but it required longer listening on both sides. The outcome was worth all of it.

In your personal life, what would it take for you to practice listening longer and hearing what is said before you respond? If you've not done it much, you will probably need to practice and develop that listening muscle. Instead of assuming you know what the other person is going to say anyway, why not actually listen with a more open mind and a bit of grace? Imagine if our children, as they grow up in our home, felt heard and understood even when they didn't get what they wanted. What about the workplace or classroom? Neighbors and friends? I'm ashamed to admit the number of times I have judged people by what I assumed about them based on their appearance, language, or friends. Over and over, I have experienced an "aha" moment when I finally heard their story and could see them with grace. How amazing it would be if I assumed the best even before I knew the whole story, and then listened longer?

I invite you to join me on a campaign to be quick to listen, slow to speak, and slow to get angry. Whatever our differences, and they are many, I pray that our words would be saturated with grace and understanding and lead us to peace.

Further Reading

James 1:19-20 *Understand this, my dear brothers and sisters: You must all be quick to listen, slow to speak, and slow to get angry. Human anger does not produce the righteousness God desires.*

James 1:26 *If you claim to be religious but don't control your tongue, you are fooling yourself, and your religion is worthless.*

Proverbs 13:3 *Those who control their tongue will have a long life, opening your mouth can ruin everything.*

Proverbs 18:15 *Intelligent people are always ready to learn. Their ears are open for knowledge.*

Proverbs 21:23 *Watch your tongue and keep your mouth shut, and you will stay out of trouble.*

James 3:3-12 *We can make a large horse go wherever we want by means of a small bit in its mouth. And a small rudder makes a huge ship turn wherever the pilot chooses to go, even though the winds are strong. In the same way, the tongue is a small thing that makes grand speeches. But a tiny spark can set a great forest on fire. And among all the parts of the body, the tongue is a flame of fire. It is a whole world of wickedness, corrupting your entire body. It can set your whole life on fire, for it is set on fire by hell itself. People can tame all kinds of animals, birds, reptiles, and fish, but no one can tame the tongue. It is restless and evil, full* *of deadly poison. Sometimes it praises our Lord and Father, and sometimes it curses those who have been made in the image of God. And so blessing and cursing come pouring out of the same mouth. Surely, my brothers and sisters, this is not right! Does a spring of water bubble out with both fresh water and bitter water? Does a fig tree produce olives, or a grapevine produce figs? No, and you can't draw fresh water from a salty spring.*

[Communication, Habits, Relationships, Trust]

Chapter 48

A Snapshot of....

SPECS AND FOCUS

The year 2020 hit with a bang. A worldwide pandemic, racial violence and inequity were in the news daily. A volatile election year and the quarantine scrambled our lives almost beyond recognition. How should we respond? More importantly, how do we survive?

I was talking with someone about the untimely death of a mutual friend from ALS. Not fair. She had lost a son right before being diagnosed. Too much. For a person, for a family, for a community. I have a dear friend just diagnosed with aggressive cancer. Another friend just lost her brother, a wonderful young man with a wife and four chil-

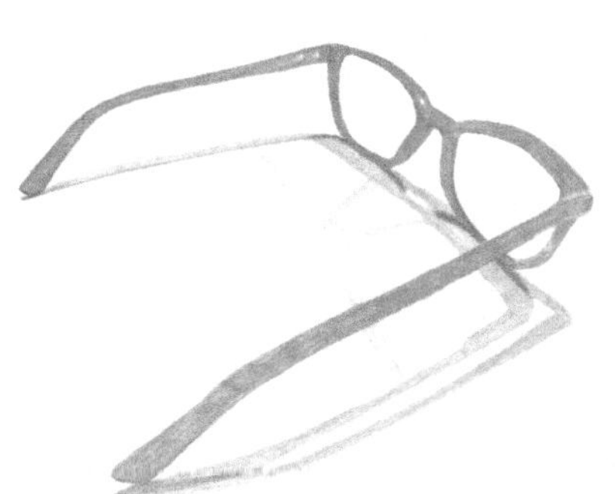

dren. *Too much!* How do we cope? Surviving may be possible, but what about thriving?

Years ago, I was struck with the question, "What are you looking at?" In the stuff of daily life, where are you focusing your attention? I submit that whatever holds your attention is defining the quality of your life. Someone close to me despises a certain political figure. Despises. What does she do for a few hours a day? She watches the news until her blood boils and her hair falls out (figuratively speaking, of course). It's one thing to be informed on critical issues, it's another to fill your head and heart with details that don't help. What are you giving your attention to over all other things? That person, problem, or issue is going to filter your perception of just about every aspect of life.

I am not suggesting we bury our heads in the sand and live ignorant of the world around us, but we don't have to give culture or news writers the power to define us. They are not infallible. There are challenges we must face and respond to, but we don't have to live in them. They don't have to solely define us.

During Covid it became the norm to see drive-by graduations and birthday parties. There were online weddings. Grandparents saw new grandbabies through windows, unable to touch or hold them. Extroverts started developing ticks or got famous on Tik Tok and introverts forgot how to hold a conversation. This was our new normal. But what we choose to focus on goes beyond just Covid and politics, it determines how we see and perceive our whole life. It will make us resentful or grateful.

I realize that it is much easier to say "Only focus on goodness" than it is to practice it every day. There is a lot going on in the world and much of it isn't good. In fact, the bad may outweigh the good in your life today, but we must remember that our thoughts are not beyond our control. Granted, any thought may enter your mind, but you get to decide whether it lives there or gets sent back to where it came from (not heaven).

Three tools may help in this area:

— First, choose to control your thoughts. Be the boss. When your thoughts are running amok and dragging you into fear or despair or bitterness, say no. Choose to guide your mind to helpful, hopeful, and fruitful thinking. (I have come to see my mind as a toddler who must constantly be taught how to play nice.)

> *And now, dear brothers and sisters, one final thing. Fix your thoughts on what is true, and honorable, and right, and pure, and lovely, and admirable. Think about things that are excellent and worthy of praise.* (Phil 4:8)

— Secondly, practice gratitude. Focus on what is good in your life. Are you healthy? Roof over your head? Food in the cupboard? Does somebody love you, even just one person? In the 70s there was a very popular song by Chaka Khan and Rufus called *Tell Me Something Good*. That's what I'm talking about. Tell yourself something good!

— Finally, give your mind good things to focus on. Choose wisely what you watch on media and what you read. You are feeding your brain information all the time. Make it count!

Life is a hodgepodge of good, bad, and ugly. Decide today what will hold the bulk of your attention, your time, and your thoughts. You get to choose where to direct your heart today. Point it toward something that gives you life and doesn't drain it from you. Choose hope.

So, what are you looking at? What most grabs your focus? Is it what you don't have or is it gratitude for what you do have? With friends and family, are you focusing on their faults and shortcomings or on what makes them almost loveable? Are your thoughts about God based on His Word or on your perception of His lack of action in your life? If you are spending hours of your day reading and watching the news, perhaps you could take a break. Look at a tree. Call a friend. Send someone a note of encouragement. Remember, whatever you're focusing most of your attention on is defining the quality of your life right now.

Further Reading

Colossians 3:15-17 *And let the peace that comes from Christ rule in your hearts. For as members of one body you are called to live in peace. And always be thankful. Let the message about Christ, in all its richness, fill your lives. Teach and counsel each other with all the wisdom he gives. Sing psalms and hymns and spiritual songs to God with thankful hearts. And whatever you do or say, do it as a representative of the Lord Jesus, giving thanks through him to God the Father.*

1 Thessalonians 5:18 *Be thankful in all circumstances, for this is God's will for you who belong to Christ Jesus.*

2 Corinthians 10:5 *We demolish arguments and every pretension that sets itself up against the knowledge of God, and we take captive every thought to make it obedient to Christ.*

Romans 8:5 *Those who are dominated by the sinful nature think about sinful things, but those who are controlled by the Holy Spirit think about things that please the Spirit.*

[Gratitude, Hope, Perspective]

Chapter 49

A Snapshot of....

MIRACULOUS PAINTS

When my kids were little, I found a new kind of coloring book. All you needed in order to paint was water. You dip your brush in the water, stroke the brush on the page, and "Voilá!" the picture would come alive with color. Embedded in the lines of the drawing was paint that only appeared when you applied the water to it. The brilliance of this book was that there was no paint on furniture, clothing or faces, or at least not as much. (I'm sure you artists find this to be a terrible idea that limits creativity. True, but stay with me for the sake of the snapshot.)

In my life and in conversation with others, I find that people without love are like the pages of those coloring books. There is the potential for beauty and color, but it remains embedded in the outline of their life. People who have not been loved or who don't know how to love never seem to capture the joy and possibility that comes only through relationships. Yes, people can be challenging and disappointing, but so are you. Love is what allows all of us strange, complicated, unfinished people to come alive and thrive.

Since we are limited in our ability to love perfectly, it seems obvious to me that we are desperate for a love that can turn our black-and-white existence into living color. My sisters and I were loved well by Mom. Honestly, everything she did was for us: she fed us, clothed us, and kept a roof over our heads. That required her working a minimum of two jobs at a time, which meant we spent a lot of time taking care of each other. I adore my sisters. I love them so much. But I'm guessing my love was somewhat less than perfect as I tried to rule the house in Mom's absence. (No, no one asked me to take over, it was my gift to them.) As I grew up and discovered how imperfect my love was and how deeply I needed a healing love, I slowly learned to let God's love seep into the most broken and hurt places. His love is powerful, but my resistance was high because I'd learned in childhood how to protect myself. The problem is that we end up living black-and-white lives when color is just below the surface waiting to be set free.

C.S. Lewis wrote about this in *The Weight of Glory*,

> "It would seem that Our Lord finds our desires not too strong, but too weak. We are half-hearted creatures, fooling about with drink and sex and ambition when infinite joy is offered us, like an ignorant child who wants to go on making mud pies in a slum because he cannot imagine what is meant by the offer of a holiday at the sea. We are far too easily pleased."

In my years of counseling, I've talked to so many people who are "okay" with their life as it is because it's better than it was or it's "good enough." I get that. But just as the first blush of romantic love can transform our world, the love of God touches everything and colors it with hope and life in even greater ways. I don't know your story, but I know we're all in the market for peace and healing, or maybe just a way to expand our limited expectations so we experience our very best life.

Perhaps you used to think a lot about God but don't anymore, or maybe you've never even considered Him. Possibly you are someone experiencing God's love every day. Whatever your situation, I invite you, encourage you, to turn your heart and thoughts toward Him today. Even just a "Hey, God" can be a start to turning our attention to the One who loves us beyond understanding. Nobody on this planet thinks you're as awesome as God does. Surely that's worth a conversation, right?

Start small or go big, but begin to practice courage and invite God to show you how loved you are and what you are created for. Your life is a kaleidoscope of living color.

Further Reading

Ephesians 3:17-19 *Then Christ will make his home in your hearts as you trust in him. Your roots will grow down into God's love and keep you strong. And may you have the power to understand, as all God's people should, how wide, how long, how high, and how deep his love is. May you experience the love of Christ, though it is too great to understand fully. Then you will be made complete with all the fullness of life and power that comes from God.*

Romans 8:35-37 *Can anything ever separate us from Christ's love? Does it mean he no longer loves us if we have trouble or calamity, or are persecuted, or hungry, or destitute, or in danger, or threatened with death?... No, despite all these things, overwhelming victory is ours through Christ, who loved us.*

John 3:16-18 MSG *This is how much God loved the world: He gave his Son, his one and only Son. And this is why: so that no one need be destroyed; by believing in him, anyone can have a whole and lasting life. God didn't go to all the trouble of sending his Son merely to point an accusing finger, telling the world how bad it was. He came to help, to put the world right again. Anyone who trusts in him is acquitted; anyone who refuses to trust him has long since been under the death sentence without knowing it. And why? Because of that person's failure to believe in the one-of-a-kind Son of God when introduced to him.*

Ephesians 2:4,5 *But God is so rich in mercy, and he loved us so much, that even though we were dead because of our sins, he gave us life when he raised Christ from the dead. (It is only by God's grace that you have been saved!)*

1 John 3:16-17 MSG *This is how we've come to understand and experience love: Christ sacrificed his life for us. This is why we ought to live sacrificially for our fellow believers, and not just be out for ourselves. If you see some brother or sister in need and have the means to do something about it but turn a cold shoulder and do nothing, what happens to God's love? It disappears. And you made it disappear.*

[Faith, Love, Relationships, Restoration]

Chapter 50

A Snapshot of....

A Better GPS

I vividly remember the first time I saw a GPS (Global Positioning System). I was at a family reunion in Tennessee and my uncle and I snuck off to play golf. He had a Garmin device in his car and punched in the address of the golf course. Could that really work? A female voice began to tell us to turn left in five hundred feet then go straight three miles. At one point, we missed one of the turns and the device beeped once and her voice intoned, "Recalculating." After a few seconds she directed us to "Turn left in one hundred feet." Well, we were already a hundred feet further along and missed that turnoff too. "Recalculating." This happened a few

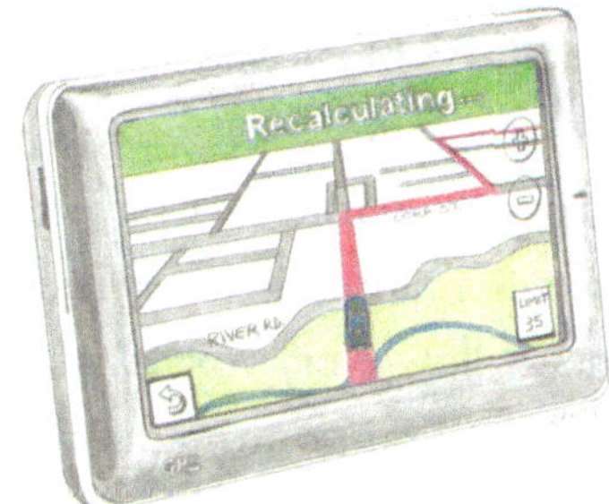

times on our quest to find the golf course. It may have been my imagination, but I sensed a certain edge to her voice after a couple of recalculations.

Today, this technology is much more advanced and comes standard in most vehicles, and many of us would be lost without it. I can't help but think about GPS in the figurative sense. What is the guidance system each of us uses in life? What directs us to the destination we desire? Whether that's simply living in peace or being king/queen of the world, what is directing our daily choices and plans? We all have something or someone whose voice guides us.

It is easy to succumb to the voices I hear on TV, radio, or social media, telling me who I should be, what I should do and how I should live. The problem is, they don't agree with each other! What's a body to do? Well, friend, you'd better figure out which voice has your highest good in mind, knows you best, and wants goodness for you.

May I make a suggestion? I've talked with people who were guided by the voice of a parent long after the parent was gone, and they were fully adulted with kids of their own. They still lived in fear of doing the wrong thing, a deep sense of inadequacy, or confidence that they were doomed to fail—all based on the words spoken to them in childhood. Some folks I know are fully tuned in to the GPS of success as defined by our culture, which means status and money. For some, it is their addiction to food, sex, drugs, or you-name-it. I have talked with people who consider themselves a failure because they don't have a spouse or children and they follow every voice that promises to get them there. While we all have disappointments stemming from unfulfilled dreams or failures, what do we allow to drive our decisions, plans, and goals on a daily basis?

I am a person who has worked a lot throughout my life to make and keep people happy. I like it when people are happy, safe and at peace. Yes, I know that I don't have the power to do that for the world, but Lord knows I've tried. Whatever it is that has driven me over the years, I have discovered two very important truths: I ain't God but there is One. I am learning to listen for His voice as best I can and let that be my GPS. I'm not talking about micro-decisions like, "Dear God, shall I wear the red shirt or the blue one?" I'm talking about getting to know God more every day and learning the big stuff: how He created us to live our best life in relationship with Him and with grace and love toward others. This is no small task but it has proven to be the way to a life that brings peace, hope, and joy. Not a bad destination.

My uncle and I did find the golf course and had a lot of fun that day. I am grateful for the voice that led us there and for "her" patience as we progressed with fits and starts. She knew her stuff and we were rewarded by following her guidance. How much greater a benefit in listening to God's voice as He guides and tells us to "recalculate." Good lesson there, eh?

Further Reading

Psalm 23:2 *He lets me rest in green meadows; he leads me beside peaceful streams.*

Psalm 25:9 *He leads the humble in doing right, teaching them his way.*

Psalm 48:14 *For that is what God is like. He is our God forever and ever, and he will guide us until we die.*

Psalm 73:24 *You guide me with your counsel, leading me to a glorious destiny.*

Isaiah 30:21 *Your own ears will hear him. Right behind you a voice will say, "This is the way you should go," whether to the right or to the left.*

Luke 1:78-79 *Because of God's tender mercy, the morning light from heaven is about to break upon us, to give light to those who sit in darkness and in the shadow of death, and to guide us to the path of peace.*

[Guidance, Identity, Trust]

Chapter 51

A Snapshot of....

A Grand Road Trip

I took a road trip from California to Florida and back, with a four-month vacation in the middle. I put approximately 7,800 miles on my brand-new car. I had three different travel buddies who proved to be easy companions, with patience for my driving (I am an excellent driver with an occasional attitude flare.) We ate at some very interesting establishments, avoiding chain restaurants (to create new experiences and better stories). We stayed

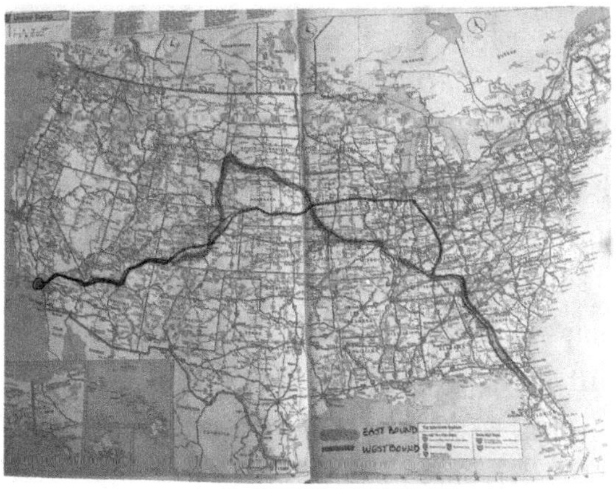

with friends or in hotels—a few questionable and one stellar, hotel, that is, in Lincoln, Nebraska. The best nights were spent with friends, enjoying their company and incredible hospitality. We traversed hot arid deserts and vast mountain ranges, crossed rivers and wound our way through forests. We navigated city traffic and spent countless hours flying across plains where we saw few other cars. We drove through days of clear blue skies, heavy gray clouds, dense fog, light rain, heavy rain, and snow—sometimes on the same day. It's one country, several states and as varied as you can imagine.

After four months in Florida slowing my life and driving a golf cart most of the time, then a road trip with no time constraints, Los Angeles was culture shock: everyone in a hurry, cars buzzing about, and everybody crabby and impatient, especially me.

Here's the thing: life is like a long road trip. We sometimes navigate rough terrain and bad weather, while other days are sunshine and breathtaking vistas. There will be lonely seasons ("No Signal") and others filled with people we love. There are situations where I know I am not up to the task, I just can't do it, and days where it feels like I can do anything. On this road trip of life, we experience all of it, no matter who we are or how awesome we believe ourselves to be.

Upon returning to LA, I had to navigate a new season of life: turning a house into a home, caring for Mom's needs, finding a rhythm for self-care, and discerning God's desire for my life. It helps me to think of my days in terms of a road trip. Each day is different. Some are disappointing, like driving ten hours out of our way to see Mt. Rushmore and finding it completely shrouded in fog. Others are glorious, like getting up the next morning and going back to find the great sculpture stunningly clear against a blue sky. The tough days we get through (with grit and God's help) and the glorious days we drink in and let fill up our souls. We learn to spend more time with people who fill us up and less time with those who drain us.

These days I am working at taking each day as it comes, choosing to slow down, minimize calendar clutter, and invest in the people who matter to me. I am working to become more aware of God in the big and little things, and working toward a vacation kind of attitude. And may we remember that the road can feel endless and tiresome some days, and a grand adventure the next.

Further Reading

Ecclesiastes 3:1-8 *For everything there is a season, a time for every activity under heaven. A time to be born and a time to die. A time to plant and a time to harvest. A time to kill and a time to heal. A time to tear down and a time to build up. A time to cry and a time to laugh. A time to grieve and a time to dance. A time to scatter stones and a time to gather stones. A time to embrace and a time to turn away. A time to search and a time to quit searching. A time to keep and a time to throw away. A time to tear and a time to mend. A time to be quiet and a time to speak. A time to love and a time to hate. A time for war and a time for peace.*

Ecclesiastes 9:7 *So go ahead. Eat your food with joy, and drink your wine with a happy heart, for God approves of this!*

Galatians 5:22-23 *But the Holy Spirit produces this kind of fruit in our lives: love, joy, peace, patience, kindness, goodness, faithfulness, gentleness, and self-control. There is no law against these things!*

Isaiah 61:1-2 *The Spirit of the Sovereign LORD is upon me, for the LORD has anointed me to bring good news to the poor. He has sent me to comfort the brokenhearted and to proclaim that captives will be released and prisoners will be freed. He has sent me to tell those who mourn that the time of the LORD's favor has come, and with it, the day of God's anger against their enemies.*

Jeremiah 31:13 *The young women will dance for joy, and the men—old and young—will join in the celebration. I will turn their mourning into joy. I will comfort them and exchange their sorrow for rejoicing.*

[Attitude, Choices, Daily Life]

Chapter 52

A Snapshot of …

A Jar of Rocks

In the days following my husband's death, I thought a lot about what I'd say at his memorial service. Fact is, Budd was a good guy. It's also a fact that we had some difficult years. I have been a part of services where the deceased should have been bequeathed sainthood judging from the stories of their endless patience, love, humility, grace, etc. Like I said, Budd was a good guy, but he wasn't perfect. Between us we had an impressive list of broken places, enough to hurt a marriage for sure. He was also very funny, loved his family more than anything, and worked hard to provide for us.

I wanted to say what was most true of his good character without petitioning for his sainthood. I wanted to be honest and to honor the real Budd—the human one. As I prayerfully pondered, I was struck with a picture of a jar filled with rocks. There were larger rocks in the bottom and many, many smaller rocks on top. With Budd's death it was as though the jar was shaken very hard. The smaller rocks sifted to the bottom, revealing the large rocks which represented the things that I loved most about him, the traits that had caused me to fall in love with him in the first place. Smaller rocks were the irritations, hurts, and failures that had accumulated over the years of our marriage. Because of unforgiveness, bitterness, and brokenness, I had allowed these smaller rocks to cover what was most important between us.

Budd's memorial service was wonderful. Seriously. There was much laughter and plenty of tears. Budd was a good-hearted man with a twisted and delightful sense of humor. Our kids were able to share stories of their father that perfectly reflected his love, provision, and quirks. It was a celebration of a human life—not a saint, you understand, but a good human being, father, friend, and husband.

In a broader context, this snapshot impacts work relationships, friendships, extended family, and more. We have the power to choose what we will focus on. There are families where siblings or parents and children have lost any sense of connection or relationship. (I do not include abuse in this example as there are extenuating circumstances that must be dealt with in extremely dysfunctional family systems.) A friend's mother was in the hospital on hospice care. They had been estranged and he was hesitant to visit his mom and subject himself to more rejection or judgment.

I encouraged him to visit his mom if only to say good-bye. I offered to go with him if it would help. He put it off until one day at work he told me his mom had passed away. Nothing had been resolved. Weeks later, months later, and even years later he would tell me again that he wished he had gone to the hospital even just one time. Please understand, this is not about ignoring hurt or abuse, but it is also not allowing that hurt and abuse to control our life for all of our days.

The hopeful note in all of this is that as I look back over the last half of our marriage, I could see where Budd and I had worked hard to retrieve the big rocks. Whether through counseling, intentional connection, or forgiveness—usually all three—we had embarked on a recovery mission, and it had paid dividends. I didn't need to grieve pure failure on our part, but rather accept what was true of two broken people trying to build a family and a home. In the seasons where we gave the little rocks center stage, we fought a lot and were quite isolated from one another. As we gained a correct perspective, we began to see that we were good together, we had two fabulous kids who were good adults and good people.

Every once in a while, when things are strained, shake the jar. You may be surprised by what you find there.

Further Reading

John 15:12-13 *This is my commandment: Love each other in the same way I have loved you. There is no greater love than to lay down one's life for one's friends.*

1 Peter 4:8 *Most important of all, continue to show deep love for each other, for love covers a multitude of sins.*

1 John 3:16 *We know what real love is because Jesus gave up his life for us. So we also ought to give up our lives for our brothers and sisters.*

Luke 6:30-32 *Give to anyone who asks; and when things are taken away from you, don't try to get them back. Do to others as you would like them to do to you. "If you love only those who love you, why should you get credit for that? Even sinners love those who love them!"*

[Grace, Grief, Perspective, Relationships]

Chapter 53

A Snapshot of....

ADRIFT OR AT REST

Years ago, I was invited to take a sailboat ride. It was amazing. When the breeze catches the sail, it is breathtaking. The captain and crew knew just what to move, open, or tie down. It was like watching a beautiful sort of dance. We would catch the breeze and be pushed forward across the water. At one point the wind went very still. I thought, "Oh no...what happens now?" For a short time, we just lazily drifted, had a snack, and talked about how beautiful the day was. A short while later the

Exodus 31:15a *You have six days each week for your ordinary work, but the seventh day must be a Sabbath day of complete rest, a holy day dedicated to the* L*ORD.*

[Peace, Rest, Sabbath]

Topical Index

While I believe that Snapshots will give people specific help or encouragement depending on their needs or unique way of thinking, I thought it might be helpful to offer a topical guide. Sometimes we are in a season or circumstance that requires certain focus. I hope this helps.

TOPIC CHAPTERS

Knowing God

There are a lot of religions and denominations in the world, and I thought it might be good to clarify what I mean by hearing and trusting God. A foundation of my faith is belief that the Bible is true and it is sacred. After all these many years of believing in God, my faith today is based on experience as well as Scripture. God has proven Himself faithful, present and loving through even the toughest challenges in my life. I do not doubt Him or His goodness.

God created everything and He created it perfect. Human beings, given the ability to choose how they would live, chose their own way and walked away from God. The results were disastrous. God is perfect and we are not, which leaves a break in relationship. Since none of us can become perfect by ourselves, God chose to pay the price for what the Bible calls sin (separation from God) by sending His Son, Jesus, as a man to live and die on earth. While it sounds like a fantasy story, its true. Simply by believing that God loves you and believing that Jesus made a way for you to be in relationship with the God who created you, you are offered new life. This new life comes with God's presence and power leading to your best life.

John 3:16-18 *"This is how much God loved the world: He gave his Son, his one and only Son. And this is why: so that no one need be destroyed; by believing in him, anyone can have a whole and lasting life. God didn't go to all the trouble of sending his Son merely to point an accusing finger, telling the world how bad it was. He came to help, to put the world right again. Anyone who trusts in him is acquitted; anyone who refuses to trust him has long since been under the death sentence without knowing it. And why? Because of that person's failure to believe in the one-of-a-kind Son of God when introduced to him."*

Ephesisans 2:7-10 *Now God has us where he wants us, with all the time in this world and the next to shower grace and kindness upon us in Christ Jesus. Saving is all his idea, and all his work. All we do is trust him enough to let him do it. It's God's gift from start to finish! We don't play the major role. If we did, we'd probably go around bragging that we'd done the whole thing! No, we neither make nor save ourselves. God does both the making and saving. He creates each of us by Christ Jesus to join him in the work he does, the good work he has gotten ready for us to do, work we had better be doing."*

2 Corinthians 5:17 *"This means that anyone who belongs to Christ has become a new person. The old life is gone; a new life has begun!"* NLT

Eph 2:8-9 NLT [8] *God saved you by his grace when you believed. And you can't take credit for this; it is a gift from God.* [9] *Salvation is not a reward for the good things we have done, so none of us can boast about it.*

Full disclosure, it doesn't mean your life becomes perfect. You still have to be human and live on this crazy planet. But you will never be alone and when you die, your eternity is secured in God's kingdom. It's your best life today and forever.

Acknowledgements

How do I say thank you? This book would not exist without the prayers, pom-poms, encouragement and giftings of more people than I can mention. I believe without a doubt that God "told me" to publish it (knowing that I was ill-equipped to do so!) and has provided gifted and faithful people along this twenty-five year journey. In the earliest stages of it, without Sherry's encouragement and artwork it never would have gotten off the ground. She helped take it from a great idea to an actual project. A bit later, without Liz hounding me—literally—there would have been no initial blog or gathering of snapshots in a shareable form. She designed the website and taught me–with great patience–to get Snapshots out there through the website. In this last phase, without Elle picking up the load of figuring out how to publish it, I'd still just have a file on my computer named "Snapshots." My copy-editor Staci and typographer Latte infused order into the manuscript and hope into this author. I consider them friends, though I've never seen them face-to-face.

In addition, I have been begged, encouraged and challenged by countless friends and church members to not give up. Their words always came at my lowest points and served to help me go one more step in the process. I am grateful to my friends who prayed faithfully and believed in this project. I have been blessed with a church family who have allowed me to teach and counsel them as they shared their most honest stories, often the heart of particular Snapshots. Serving on staff at Christian Assembly has been a gift that truly keeps on giving. It is a beautiful thing to be a part of the Body of Christ.

I am so grateful to the four women—Sherry, Connie, Renee and Kim–who provided the artwork that brings life to each Snapshot. I'm tempted to just start naming names but I would certainly leave someone out and that would break my heart. I pray that God would especially bless every single person who obediently gave their encouragement or expertise. To quote the amazing Eugene Peterson, this book is nothing short of "A long obedience in the same direction."

About the Author

Kathy Christopher is a seasoned teacher, counselor, and spiritual leader whose life and ministry have been a testament to the transformative power of God's grace. With nearly 30 years of pastoral experience at Christian Assembly Church in Los Angeles, she has touched countless lives with her compassionate wisdom and deep faith. A graduate of Fuller Theological Seminary with a Master of Divinity, Kathy's ministry journey has been marked by her passion for guiding others toward healing and growth.

Her story is one of resilience and redemption. Raised in a family scarred by poverty, abuse, and hardship, Kathy openly shares how her faith in Jesus shaped her path, offering healing, comfort, and transformation through every trial. Widowed unexpectedly in 2010, she has navigated life's uncharted terrain with courage,

Connie Chandler has known me since the day I was born. She is my sister. She lives in The Villages, FL with her wonderful husband, Al, and is surrounded by great friends. Connie develops online training modules for businesses. She is an artist who works predominantly with colored pencils. Connie is one of the kindest people I know and has influenced me greatly. Thank you, Sistah, for joining in this venture!

— Connie created 'Unexpected Joy' and 'A Hard and Faithful Life'.

Kim MacDonald: Retired ESL teacher who still volunteers around the world. Loves other cultures, nature, hiking, reading fiction, playing with watercolor, and her dog Reef!

— Kim created 'A Seething Volcano' and 'Deep Roots'.

Images created from my pictures are:

— A Dump Truck of Hope

— Red Mary Janes

— An Unfortunate Win

— A Desperate Grasp

— A Grand Road Trip

Made in the USA
Coppell, TX
16 February 2026

71712594R10144